The ~~Marketing~~ Plan

also by Malcolm H B McDonald

Marketing Plans:
How to prepare them, how to use them

with John W Leppard

How to Sell a Service:
Guidelines for effective selling in a service business

Effective Industrial Selling

The Marketing Plan

A pictorial guide for managers

Malcolm H B McDonald and Peter Morris

Heinemann Professional Publishing

Heinemann Professional Publishing Ltd
Halley Court, Jordan Hill, Oxford OX2 8EJ
OXFORD   LONDON   MELBOURNE   AUCKLAND   SINGAPORE
IBADAN   NAIROBI   GABORONE   KINGSTON

First published 1987
Reprinted 1987, 1988, 1989 (twice)

British Library Cataloguing in Publication Data
McDonald, Malcolm H. B.
    Marketing plans: a pictorial guide.
    1 Marketing—Management
    I. Title   II. Morris, Peter
    658.8'02   RF5415.13

ISBN 0 434 91223 9

Printed in Great Britain by
Hartnolls Limited, Bodmin, Cornwall

Contents

Introduction

After more than half a century of marketing theory and practice, marketing planning still remains one of the great, unconquered challenges.

This challenge continues to grow as the environment in which organisations operate becomes increasingly hostile, abrasive and dynamic. Indeed there is one view which believes that it is this very turbulence which somehow makes planning a pointless exercise, for surely the world is moving on at too fast a pace to be planning for five, three, or even two years ahead.

But against this view, there is a growing body of evidence to show that the difference between efficiency and effectiveness (or in planning terms, the difference between tactics and strategy) is becoming more, not less important. Today, successful chief executives are grasping the absolute necessity of understanding where their companies should be going, with this direction properly articulated in plans that identify and develop those things that make

a company significantly and profitably different over time. It is not difficult to spot those organisations that have not adopted this strategic planning orientation. They reorganise with regular monotony, and more and more such firms are being taken over by more enterprising firms that have learned to drive using the strategic planning approach. Such marketing planning will never be easy. Indeed, it grows more difficult by the day.

It is our most sincere hope that this book's unique approach to this complex subject will both aid understanding and at the same time encourage readers to delve deeper into the subject, for example by reading *Marketing Plans: how to prepare them; how to use them* (Heinemann 1984).

We hope you find this book interesting, amusing and, above all, useful.

Malcolm McDonald
Peter Morris
April 1987

Chapter 1
Understanding the Marketing Process

In the business jungle there is a clearing. The natives call it the Market Place.

Here those with goods chase those with money, and those with money chase those with goods. . .

. . . until they catch each other. Unfortunately it is not always so.

Sometimes those with the goods search in vain for those with the money, and vice versa. Some magic is needed to bring them together.

We call this magic MARKETING.

What is this marketing magic?

I'LL GIVE YOU THIS IF YOU GIVE ME THAT

Is it selling, perhaps? Selling with a University degree?

BUY ONE

Or is it just another name for advertising?

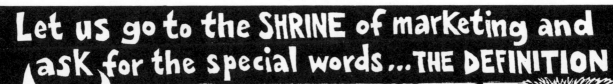

Let us go to the SHRINE of marketing and ask for the special words... THE DEFINITION

MARKETING JU-JU

The creative management function which promotes trade and employment by assessing customer needs and initiates research and development to meet them. It co-ordinates the resource of production and distribution of goods and services, determines and directs the nature and scale of the total effort required to sell profitably to the ultimate user.

OR: Finding out what the customer wants

... and providing it.

Simple enough

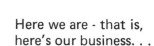

Here we are - that is, here's our business. . .

... and here's our customer.

All we've got to do is find out what he or she wants

... and deliver.

BUSINESS ENVIRONMENT

This then is the essence of the marketing process. But we mustn't forget the jungle all around - the **business environment**

Competition lurks behind every tree...

and the technological advantages enjoyed by some competitors might prove decisive in the fight for survival.

Non-drip mud means that the job can get done faster...

and unskilled people can use it without getting in a mess.

Which means that it can be sold in supermarketplaces instead of the old specialist trading posts. Distribution is profoundly affected....

Then, after the competition and the technology we come to the raw material - the trees and the mud from which the goods are made.

3

There's the labour force needed to keep the businesses going....

...and the prevailing financial climate, which affects everybody.

Also, there's government legislation, which could help - or equally hinder - the performances of individual businesses.

All these things....

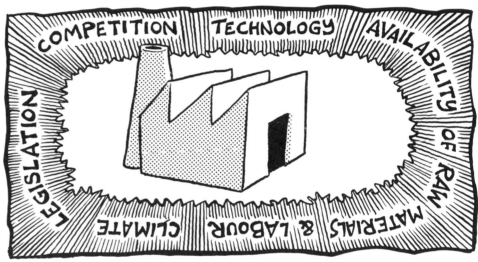

COMPETITION TECHNOLOGY AVAILABILITY OF RAW MATERIALS & LABOUR CLIMATE LEGISLATION

are *outside* factors over which the business has no control. They make up the BUSINESS ENVIRONMENT.

They make the environment *dynamic* - ever changing. But what about those things over which the business does have some control?

For instance, what strong points does the business have? Each has its own unique set of skills and limitations, so with luck we do what we're best at...

...but this may not be possible if nobody wants what we can do.

4

When traditional markets go into decline, it's necessary to change, which some people find difficult or impossible. They become less competitive, whereas those who can match their capabilities to customers' needs become more competitive. You must change your skills - or move your business to where your old skills are still needed. Your business is one thing over which you have some control.

Another area where you have some control is here - the customer. There is a myth about this mysterious being...

...which is that his needs can be manipulated by powerful business interests.

The failure rate of all new products launched explodes that one.

But what *are* customers' needs and how do we fulfill them?

THE NEEDS REMAIN CONSTANT - THE WAYS OF SATISFYING THEM CHANGE

For instance, people have always needed home entertainment - which sold pianos in Victorian times...

5

...and TV sets more recently.

TV is simply a new way of satisfying an age-old need.

In the end the customer has the final say. All customers have different ways of satisfying their needs, and when they have the choice they will choose the product or service which they perceive as offering the greatest benefits at the price.

Because of this basic fact a firm's performance can only be measured in terms of

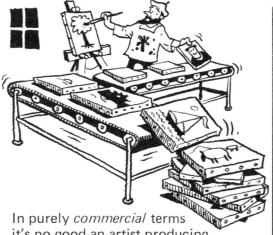

In purely *commercial* terms it's no good an artist producing ten pictures a day if he doesn't sell any...

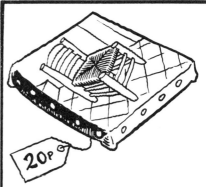

...and cheapness is no criterion either, since if no-one wants his work no-one will be prepared to spend anything on it.

So... You have to produce what the customer wants... This is true of all commercial operations

There must be enough customers (sales) to tip the balance or the company will go broke.

Increased production - increased efficiency - would only mean more goods on the shelves, not more sales. So the answer lies in the market place.

But what's *The Market Place?*

Is it your customer, surrounded by competitive products and services? Partly. In fact, it's not one market but many, all of them different.

e.g.

THE AIRLINE MARKET

PASSENGERS → SCHEDULED / CHARTER

FREIGHT → SCHEDULED / CHARTER

Each market is divided into

Market Segments

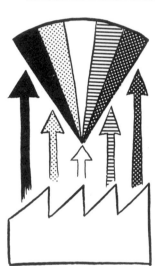

The company's capabilities must match different segments of customers' needs.

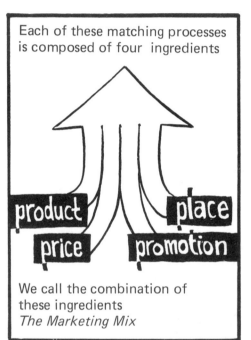

Each of these matching processes is composed of four ingredients

product   place
price   promotion

We call the combination of these ingredients *The Marketing Mix*

The Marketing Mix

To meet the customers' needs we must develop *products* to satisfy them, charge the right *price,* get the goods to the right *place* (making sure the product is available when needed), and we must make the existence of the product known through *promotion*.

COMPETITION   TECHNOLOGY

LEGISLATION

Business   Marketing Mix   Market Segments

CLIMATE   MATERIALS & LABOUR   AVAILABILITY OF RAW

The components of every marketing plan are these:
  the capabilities of the individual business
  the marketing mix
  the various customer groups comprising the market segments
  an ever-changing business environment.

Summary of Chapter 1

The focal point of all activities of any organization should be the wants and needs of its customers. This is known as a marketing orientation, which is a matching between the organization's human, financial and physical resources and customer needs. This matching takes place against the background of a dynamic environment, which includes socio-economic uncertainties, legal and political constraints, technological and institutional change, and direct and indirect competition.

This matching is often undertaken for an organization by a formalized marketing department. The senior executive and his team with responsibility for the function of marketing plans, coordinates and controls the *product*, the *price*, the way in which the product is *promoted*, and the *place* where it is made available. In so doing, he is concerned not only with the separate effects of these four 'P's, but also their interactive effects, often referred to as the marketing mix.

REMEMBER THE INGREDIENTS OF A MARKETING PLAN ARE:

- The Business
- Marketing Mix
- Market Segments
- Environment

Chapter 2
The Marketing Planning Process : I

At the start of the marketing planning process the people responsible for making policy decisions have to find out certain things.

What are they selling?... to whom?.... What kind of business are they in anyway?

WE AGREE THAT WHAT WE WANT IS ...

When they have answered these questions the decision-makers will agree on a number of corporate objectives.

Although, of course, the timescale for change varies from company to company, e.g. firms in the motor industry don't expect their corporate plans to come to fruition for perhaps 10 years, while pop music companies expect a profit in a matter of months.

These corporate objectives, usually expressed in financial terms, give an account of what the company is striving to become in, say, five years time.

But, whatever the industry, corporate planners must take a number of factors into account - the expectations of shareholders, competition, the company's strengths and weaknesses, resources, etc. Essentially, the aim is to make money.

So the corporate objectives will be couched in financial terms: turnover, profit before tax, return on investment, etc. But to end up with a workable corporate plan, companies have first to gather information about their current operations. They use a series of AUDITS.

CORPORATE OBJECTIVES

These are the audits which might be carried out by a production company, one for each function of the organisation. The audits should provide answers to questions like "Will the company be able to meet corporate objectives with its current resources and in current markets?" This will mean that each audit must suggest certain objectives and strategies of its own.

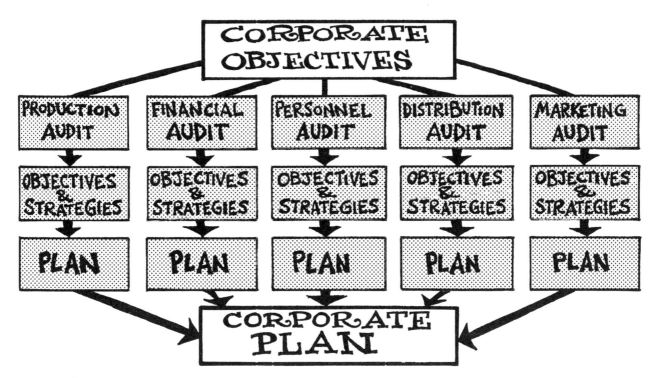

The result in each area will be a plan for realising the individual set of objectives and for implementing the particular strategy in each area, with approximate revenues and costs, and with the first year of the plan worked out in detail. These plans are agreed and then co-ordinated into one corporate plan. This book is concerned with just one part of this co-ordinated plan, the development of a marketing plan. But first let's look at some of the difficulties encountered in producing objectives and strategies - difficulties experienced by all parts of the organisation.

The corporate financial objectives have indicated the distant target of economic growth. A number of questions then follow.

Having identified the questions, the planners have to find a range of options, choose the best of them, identify the immediate objectives that these suggest, and cost it all out.

In principle simple. In practice rarely so. Why is this?

For one thing, there are various internal conflicts to be resolved.

Then, everybody in the process will have his own pet method of doing things.

With everyone going his own way, a coherent plan is unlikely. Also, plans must change as circumstances change, so the marketing planner must apply discipline to institutionalise the process. He must make it flexible - and he must start from scratch. Without discipline there will be disagreement on what's important - some may want to maximise revenue, others make bigger profits, and so on.

NOW LET'S LOOK AT THE MARKETING PLANNING PROCESS ITSELF

CORPORATE OBJECTIVES

MARKETING AUDIT

The first step was to define corporate financial objectives. Then came the audits. We are going to deal with the marketing audit.

This can be divided into two... the external audit and the internal audit.

THE EXTERNAL AUDIT

Business Environment

All companies exist in a business environment, which has factors over which the individual company has little or no control: competition, market size, legislation, availability of raw materials and labour, etc. Finding out about these will require an external audit.

THE INTERNAL AUDIT

WIDGETS

The operation of the company, i.e. the expertise of the workforce, the investment in plant and machinery, buildings etc. are things over which it has control. These things will require an internal audit.

THE EXTERNAL AUDIT

GIVE ME WIDGETS!

The demands of the marketplace are measured by the external audit, which should seek answers to questions like "Can we meet the demands of the marketplace without too much reorganisation?"

Then, what's the competition like?

DIDGETS

Are they a force to be reckoned with? Do they have anything you don't have?

Is Government legislation a threat....?

Daily Bread
MINISTER ANNOUNCES WIDGET BAN
Unions Incensed

....or an opportunity?

Daily Bread
MINISTER ANNOUNCES COMPULSORY WIDGETS
Unions Outraged

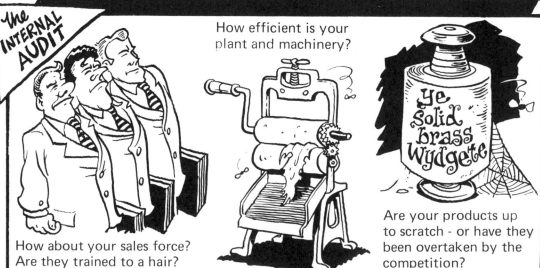

THE INTERNAL AUDIT

How about your sales force? Are they trained to a hair?

How efficient is your plant and machinery?

Ye Solid brass Wydgete

Are your products up to scratch - or have they been overtaken by the competition?

AUDITS ARE ESSENTIAL

...but who in your organisation will carry them out?

Unfortunately the ideal people are probably the busiest - the line managers. They know the job: they are involved - and they are much cheaper than outside consultants. The problem is finding the time.

They have to be given a clear idea of what you want them to do, or because they are specialists they will suffer from a kind of tunnelvision.

APPRAISAL PROCEDURES MUST BE STANDARDISED

A standard company-wide critical appraisal is needed - hence the need to institutionalise and systematise the procedures in order to make the appraisal easier.

Having done the marketing audit, the marketing planner's next move is to find out what the company's objectives and strategies in marketing must be. To do this he must analyse the information gathered by the marketing audit in something called a SWOT Analysis.

CORPORATE OBJECTIVES

MARKETING AUDIT

SWOT ANALYSIS

StrengthsWeaknesses, Opportunities, Threats

The strengths and weaknesses refer to internal characteristics of the company, while opportunities and threats are about the external factors over which the company has little control.

The SWOT analysis should be a *brief* document focussing on key factors; e.g. key differences in strengths and weaknesses between the company and its competition, and in other opportunities and threats.

A summary of reasons for bad or good performances should be included. It should be a concise, interesting analysis of the marketing audit. It is the SWOT analysis which appears in the eventual marketing plan, not the audit.

IT'S NECESSARY TO MAKE SOME ASSUMPTIONS

These assumptions are about certain external factors which will affect the company but over which it will have no control.

For example, here Mario has made the assumption that it is going to be a hot day, while Oscar is banking on it being cold. Neither will be able to tell in advance, although both will make assumptions based on past experience. Assumptions can relate to factors like over-capacity in the market, the possible effect of price levels on competition, and so on.

The problem with assumptions is that they can go wrong, so there should be as few as possible - and those that are made should be relevant.
If a marketing plan can be formulated without reference to a particular assumption, that assumption is unnecessary.

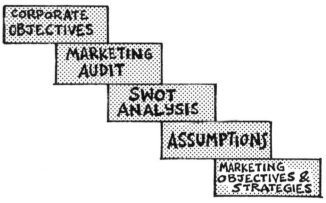

Having made the necessary assumptions about key external factors, the marketing planner is now in a position to be precise about marketing objectives and so be able to devise strategies to meet these objectives.

AN OBJECTIVE IS WHAT YOU WANT TO ACHIEVE
A STRATEGY IS HOW YOU PLAN TO ACHIEVE IT

If you can't measure an objective, how do you know when you have achieved it?

Marketing objectives are about two things only - products and markets; or rather, *permutations* of products and markets. Either existing or new products in existing markets, or existing or new products in new markets. The marketing objectives relating to these four permutations will all be different in terms of volume, value and market share.

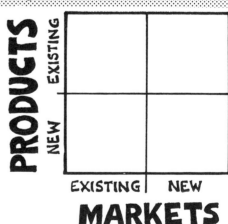

PRODUCTS (EXISTING / NEW)

EXISTING | NEW

MARKETS

The ways and means of realising objectives

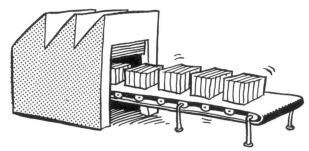

PRODUCT
PRICE
PLACE
PROMOTION

Getting the product into the customer's hands depends on the product itself, on its price, the place (policies for channel and customer service levels) and promotion (advertising, sales force, sales promotion, public relations, exhibitions etc.)

It is useful at this stage to run field tests and bring analagous experience to bear about market share, costs, profit etc. Also, consider alternative plans in case the first plan doesn't work.

I SAID WIDGETS!

FIELD TEST

The last major step in the formulation of a marketing plan is to break down the main marketing objectives and strategies into a series of sub-objectives with their own strategies. This activity is called a *programme* and it allows special emphasis to be placed on the marketing plan to take account of the particular character of the business.

For instance, in a product-based company, the overall marketing plan would be product-based, with objectives and strategies for price, place and promotion as necessary.

Whereas a geographically-based company might have a plan based on the different characteristics of the market place in different parts of the country, with objectives for price, product and promotion as necessary.

The structure of the Marketing Planning Process

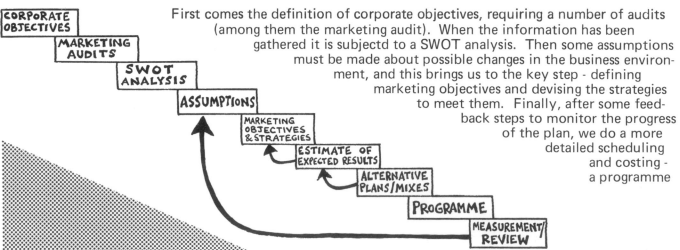

First comes the definition of corporate objectives, requiring a number of audits (among them the marketing audit). When the information has been gathered it is subjectd to a SWOT analysis. Then some assumptions must be made about possible changes in the business environment, and this brings us to the key step - defining marketing objectives and devising the strategies to meet them. Finally, after some feedback steps to monitor the progress of the plan, we do a more detailed scheduling and costing - a programme

CORPORATE OBJECTIVES
MARKETING AUDITS
SWOT ANALYSIS
ASSUMPTIONS
MARKETING OBJECTIVES & STRATEGIES
ESTIMATE OF EXPECTED RESULTS
ALTERNATIVE PLANS/MIXES
PROGRAMME
MEASUREMENT/ REVIEW

Summary of Chapter 2

It is not possible to plan a company's marketing activities in isolation from other business functions, such as production, personnel and finance. Consequently, the marketing planning process should be firmly based on a corporate planning system.

Marketing planning is the systematic application of marketing resources to achieve marketing objectives. It is the means by which an organization seeks to monitor and control the many external and internal influences on its ability to achieve profitable sales. Marketing planning also provides an understanding throughout the organization of the particular competitive stance that an organization intends to take to achieve its objectives. This helps managers of different functions to work together rather than to pursue their own functional objectives in isolation.

The marketing planning process consists of a series of steps: the marketing audit and SWOT analysis; the formulation of planning assumptions; the setting of objectives and strategies; and the development of detailed programmes of action. The key steps in the process are the setting of marketing objectives and the development of marketing strategies. Marketing objectives always express the match between products and markets; marketing strategies are the means by which the marketing objectives will be achieved.

The degree of formalization of the planning process will depend on the size and diversity of the organisation, although the planning process itself is universally applicable.

Chapter 3

The Marketing Planning Process: II

REMOVING THE myths

Why do some companies have difficulty in making marketing plans? What *are* the myths and misconceptions surrounding the marketing planning process?

WE ALREADY DO ALL THIS MARKETING STUFF WITHOUT ALL THAT MUMBO-JUMBO ABOUT OBJECTIVES & WHATSITS

This man is wrong. Probably what he's involved in is some kind of sales forecasting and budgeting.

Forecasting and Budgeting go like this.....

Hmm... LAST YEAR WE GOT 9% SALES INCREASE

First, a numerical evaluation of last year....

THIS YEAR...

Then an extrapolation....

WE'LL GET 10!

Then a target, which may or may not be realistic.

BUT WHAT ABOUT THE CANADIAN MARKET? SHUT UP!

There's no attempt to look at the market or show how to achieve sales forecasts, which

...OR DID I MEAN 11?

are often inflated to motivate the sales force to work harder,

BUT SPEND LESS!

while budgets are reduced as a safety net in case the forecasts can't be met.

The widely accepted practice is that the boss sets profit targets, decentralises the operational control so that managers are accountable for those targets - and bingo! a successful marketing plan emerges. Unfortunately there are countless examples of companies pursuing decentralised profit goals that have failed miserably.

PROFIT
The Numbers Game

SALES	UP	11%
MARGIN	UP	10%

NEVER MIND HOW... JUST DO IT!

Easier said than done.

AND I MEAN EVERYBODY

Overall volume increases and minimum rates of return are often applied to *all* markets & products regardless of market share, growth rate or the stage of a product's life cycle (see chapter 6).

Only the Bottom Line Counts

TAKE THE MONEY & RUN

Here Today Gone Tomorrow

A related problem is that these decentralised units operate only in terms of the 'bottom line'.

This is because the thinking goes:

"It's safer for managers to do what they know best - managing their *current* range of products and customers in order to meet the *current* year's budget"..

Result - a ridiculously large and varied production line, a wasteful duplication of market research, pricing muddles, confusion about the company's image, chaos and frustration - and less overall profit.

FINANCIAL OBJECTIVES

11%

I'LL GET THERE - NEVER MIND HOW!

So financial objectives are no help in determining *how* results are going to be achieved; neither are sales forecasts which are about existing products in existing markets and are expressed numerically.

MARKETING OBJECTIVES

11%

YES, BUT IN PLAIN ENGLISH, HOW?

Marketing objectives are needed to determine *how* to make a commitment to the future, which will be the only way to achieve corporate goals. But finding the right words to describe the logic of marketing objectives is more difficult than just writing down numbers.

Market Segments

Managers will not think of the relative significance of different market segments nor see the need for collection of data unless the purpose of such activities is clear. So basing the future planning of the company on sales forecasting and budgeting can be downright dangerous.

Forecasting and budgeting do not take account of the changing business environment....

...nor of the fact that the business itself changes....

....as people come and go, skills change, equipment is renewed, technology changes etc. Only through the marketing planning process can ways be found to evaluate how the business and environment interact.

Only through an audit and a SWOT analysis can the distinctive competence of the business be matched with the customer's needs.

Another myth about marketing planning is that there is no relationship between it and commercial success. The reason for this is that some individuals and companies seem to do well without planning while others with meticulous marketing plans seem to fare badly.. But when demand exceeds supply, anyone can make a profit.

AH'M JUS' A SINGIN' FOOL....

EVEN WHEN THE GOING IS GOOD, PEOPLE WITH MARKETING PLANS MAKE MORE PROFIT THAN THOSE WITHOUT

Success depends on more than competent marketing procedures

There's LUCK

I'LL BUY IT. HOW MUCH?

There's THE CRITERION OF SUCCESS

Is it wealth? Or peace of mind?

There's STYLE

WE ONLY SERVE NOBILITY

Some firms regard the quality of their custom as a measure of success.

There's CREATIVITY

BETTER MOUSE TRAP

But even geniuses need to meet customer demand. every business needs a marketing plan.

Problems encountered in making marketing plans come from the company's inability to function efficiently, and from the threats posed by the business environment. These threats are frequently difficult to anticipate.

Most managers seem most comfortable trying to deal with problems as they arise, because they are busy running the business from day to day.

Another problem is that the business is different to different people

Even if they **were** completely in favour of co-operating in the formulation of a marketing plan they would not have much time for tomorrow's problems while tackling today's.

OFFICE BOY

MANAGING DIRECTOR

and therefore everyone will have different perceptions of what it should be trying to do.

The sheer number of inside and outside issues involved make for complexity in the design and implementation of a marketing plan and for this reason a large number of companies carry on trading without coherent marketing planning. But even if the *process* itself were easy, *implementation* would still be formidably difficult because of human frailty.

For instance, if the chief executive refuses to see the need for a plan, it's virtually impossible to proceed.

And it's particularly difficult in businesses organised on the basis of divisional management who can create political difficulties

But, given top management's undivided attention, the way is clear to secure the co-operation of your colleagues in preparing a marketing plan. You'll have to show

- why a marketing plan is necessary
- why a marketing planning system is necessary
- why top management should be involved
- why the system will need testing
- why training programmes and workshops are needed
- why data must be collected, especially from remote areas of the business.

You will need a plan for planning a timetable

The co-operation of busy line managers can not be guaranteed. It's going to come as something of a shock if they are presented without warning with a thick manual on how to prepare your marketing plan.

They may lack the necessary knowledge about basic marketing principles and about the collection of essential information. The very notion of marketing planning may be incomprehensible to them.

The net result will be a bulky, useless, unreadable document which will have the effect of deterring anyone from trying again. Or if marketing planning is made an annual event, it becomes a perfunctory exercise, the plan being filed in a suitable place.

So they will picture your marketing plan as a sort of sales forecast, and they will provide their sales information in numerical form, based on present markets under the title of a marketing plan, just to satisfy you.

'Headquarters' has its own contribution to make to undermining the marketing planning process. They may regard long-term planning as essentially a Headquarters activity, and nothing to do with short-term planning, which is for operational managers. When this happens, long-term planning becomes little more than a statistical extrapolation for the benefit of the directors, while short-term planning is the familiar budgeting and sales forecast activity again.

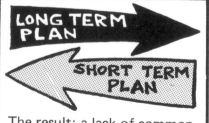

The result: a lack of common direction. And if long-term planning does not take account of the difficulties of reconciling future plans with the problems of the present operational managers will not consider alternatives to what they themselves are doing.

Headquarters may sometimes compound the crime by appointing a *planner,* whom they expect to carry out his duties in splendid isolation from the realities and problems of the line manager. In cases like this, all the problems we've just seen are magnified.

The planner is resented by the other managers and ignored by the mainstream of the business. HQ sees him as an initiator of goals and strategies rather than an initiator of planning. Without the co-operation of the operational managers he becomes a kind of HQ administration assistant, and ineffective.

Often he becomes a kind of 'piggy-in-the-middle', in an impossible political situation - and not too many executives understand marketing planning, so they will have unrealistic expectations of the planner. What's more, having appointed a marketing planner top management is relieved of the necessity of having to consider the subject again.

So, for the success of any marketing plan it is important to involve operational management in the marketing planning process and to demolish the myths around the subject.

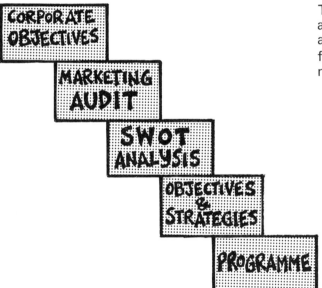

There's a proven framework for marketing planning - a process which provides a common basis for looking at the key issues facing the company and laying the foundations of co-operation between all levels of management in deciding how these can be best tackled.

By considering each step as a series of layers it is possible to apply it to all levels of management so as to produce heirarchies of marketing audits, SWOT analyses, objectives and strategies etc., both in the long- and the short-term which fit your overall purpose. Strategic and operational planning are thus linked and trade-offs and compromises between each area can be made with a greater chance of success. Only by a common understanding in all the areas of the strengths and weaknesses of the business and of the key objectives will it be possible for a feeling of common cause to be reached.

Summary of Chapter 3

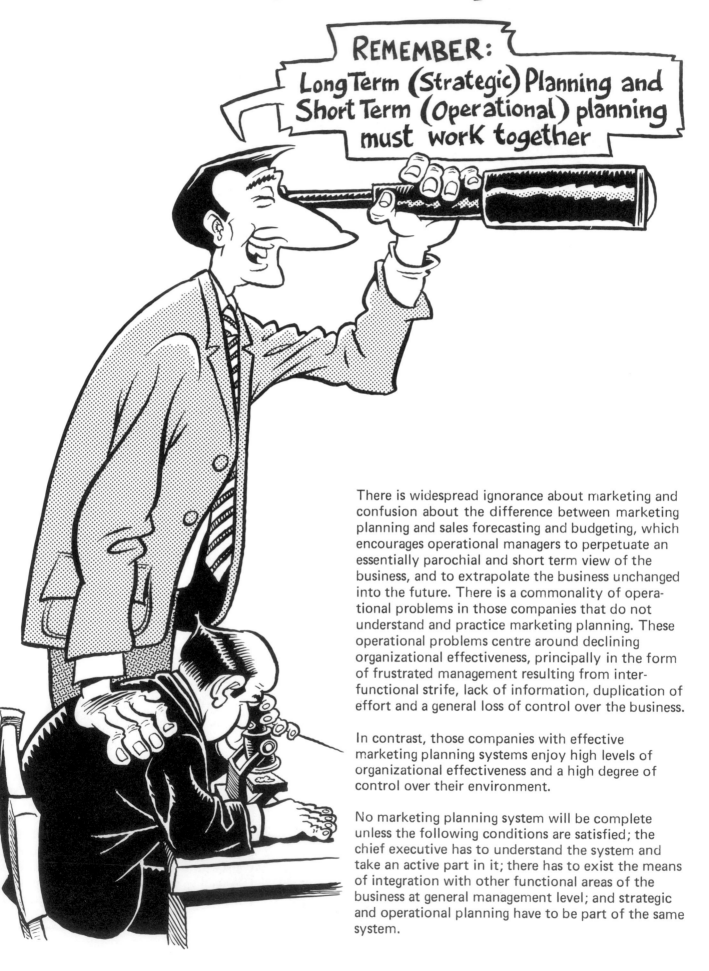

REMEMBER:
Long Term (Strategic) Planning and
Short Term (Operational) planning
must work together

There is widespread ignorance about marketing and confusion about the difference between marketing planning and sales forecasting and budgeting, which encourages operational managers to perpetuate an essentially parochial and short term view of the business, and to extrapolate the business unchanged into the future. There is a commonality of operational problems in those companies that do not understand and practice marketing planning. These operational problems centre around declining organizational effectiveness, principally in the form of frustrated management resulting from inter-functional strife, lack of information, duplication of effort and a general loss of control over the business.

In contrast, those companies with effective marketing planning systems enjoy high levels of organizational effectiveness and a high degree of control over their environment.

No marketing planning system will be complete unless the following conditions are satisfied; the chief executive has to understand the system and take an active part in it; there has to exist the means of integration with other functional areas of the business at general management level; and strategic and operational planning have to be part of the same system.

Chapter 4
The Customer and Market Audit

In this chapter we direct our gaze outward and investigate that vital band of people, our customers.

Immediately, we become aware of a distinction.

The distinction is between *customers,* who buy the goods, and *consumers,* who may or may not buy the goods they use and who may rely on the customers to supply them. An example of the distinction is the housewife who buys breakfast cereal but does not eat it herself. She's the *customer.* The cereal - eating members of her family are the *consumers.*

So, whatever·our perceptions are of the *customer* we have to be aware of the needs of the eventual *consumers.* However, for simplicity's sake going to call all of them *customers.* Most people in business know that customers are not all alike. Take the case of the prefabricated building industry.

Here are some customers.

LOCAL AUTHORITY **ARMY** **MANUFACTURER** **PROPERTY DEVELOPER**

Each of these has a different kind of requirement, which would have to be met in a different kind of way.

For Instance...

The local authority customer might want relatively cheap but attractive two-storey units for families.

The Army might want rudimentary, easy-to-erect structures...

The manufacturer might want large warehouses, the property developer luxury chalets on the Costa Brava...

The market place is not a *single* market.

Market Segment

Each market segment is made up of customers with similar *needs,* so that the segment requiring, say, temporary structures would include site engineers as well as soldiers. So, to know your market segments you have to know your customers' *needs.*

But you also have to know how many people buy *your* product instead of somebody else's; in other words, the supplier needs to know what his *share* of each market segment is, as well as knowing how many markets he's dealing with.

Next, what kind of market are you in? Here's a man selling carpets. He's in the business of selling floor coverings. Does this mean *all* floor coverings?

Well, it certainly wouldn't do for this floor. Most successful companies know how to limit their markets so that they can command a relatively large share of their market even if it's a relatively small market. This is better than having a relatively small share of a large market.

But even in one market, everything is not equal.

Some customers are better than others. In fact, 20% of the customers in any given market are responsible for 80% of the sales...

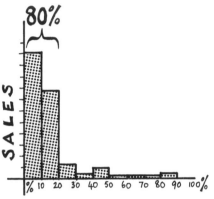

...a phenomenon known as PARETO's LAW. But before you withdraw your custom from the other four-fifths of your market, remember that your best *potential* customers might be in that group. Even if you did, the remaining 20% would obey Pareto's Law too.

So, that's what customers are like. Some buy more than others; some want high quality products; some want the lowest price, or fast delivery, and so on. What *all* customers have in common is that they obey Pareto's Law. Remember, customers can be grouped into market segments...

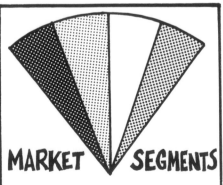

By recognising the characteristics of each segment we can make and sell products which best meet customers' specialised needs at an acceptable price - though not necessarily at the lowest price.

A company must fulfil the requirements of at least one of its market segments - that is, provide a product or series of products (or services) that the customer will find worth buying, otherwise it will find itself imitating the market leaders, trying to compete on price alone and finding the process ruinous to the business. Another reason for seeing the market in terms of market segments is that it allows the business to concentrate on what it is best at.

DO WHAT YOU'RE BEST AT...

For instance, a small company making lubricating oil might concentrate on where its expertise really lies - in making expensive oils for high technology companies, rather than taking on the multi-national companies which supply the general needs of industry.

USE THE S.W.O.T. ANALYSIS TO FIND OUT

Remember, this analysis reveals the strengths and weaknesses of the business as well as showing what the opportunities and threats of the market place are. Knowing your strengths and weaknesses will enable you to take advantage of the opportunities offered in the market segments of your business.

It's possible to analyse market segments in two ways: through *customer behaviour* and *customer attributes.*

CUSTOMER BEHAVIOUR

In analysing customer behaviour we want to answer the questions "what has he bought?" and "why did he buy it?"
"What he's bought" means the physical characteristics of the product. the volume of sales, total value, unit cost, how often bought and where from. This tells us what the market looks like.

"Why" means the degree to which the customer makes rational and irrational decisions to buy.

Irrational decisions derive from psychological and social pressures.

For instance, suppose our customer wanted to buy a car. As he looks at it in the showroom window two concepts might occur to him at once.

One is the utilitarian concept of a car as a means of transport - merely a vehicle for getting from one place to another.

The other might be the irrational concept of feeling twenty years younger...a fantasy induced by the image the car has for him.

He may ultimately be persuaded to buy a more modest vehicle by equally irrational pressures, like fear of ridicule or of seeming too ostentatious.

We can use our knowledge of customer behaviour to our marketing advantage.

When our customer looked at the car neither his rational nor his irrational concept was of a car. They were of *benefits* he imagined the car would bring....

...ease of movement plus a dashing image. Or, putting this equation into words...

YOU COULD BUY THIS CAR — WHICH MEANS THAT — YOU COULD GET FROM ONE PLACE TO ANOTHER QUICKLY — AND — CUT A DASHING FIGURE IN THE PROCESS

So a customer seeks *benefits.* Understanding what benefits are being sought will help us organise the marketing mix, the matching process which combines product, price, place and promotion in making a sale.

In the equation notice the key phrase

WHICH MEANS THAT

It translates *products* into *benefits.* In a competitive market many products have identical or similar characteristics. The salesman who can point out the benefits - as opposed to the characteristics - of his product will have established a psychological advantage over his competitors.

When a customer buys, he buys benefits:

"This car will go from 0-60 in eight seconds and cruise all day at 120 mph which means that you will get from A to B very quickly".

"This car has a very sophisticated image which means that people who own one are universally recognised as being somebody".

The phrase "which means that" embodies the principle of *benefit segmentation,* a way of looking at the marketplace in terms of benefits, of which there are three basic variations:

- STANDARD BENEFITS
- COMPANY BENEFITS
- DIFFERENTIAL BENEFITS

STANDARD BENEFITS

COMPLETE WITH FOUR WHEELS...

The simple case of translating products into benefits is an example of selling standard benefits. In the sale, every benefit should be included, however apparently obvious, e.g. "you have a choice of manual or automatic transmission, which means that you can enjoy the greater control of manual gears or the greater ease of automatic".

COMPANY BENEFITS

These stress the relationship between customer and supplier, e.g. "we offer a 24 hour delivery service, which means that you can reduce your stocks with a saving of 5% to you".

DIFFERENTIAL BENEFITS

Here the advantages of your product over others is carefully explained. "Our ball bearings are engineered to a high specification which means that you will have less down time, which means that savings on cost go up 20%".

CUSTOMER ATTRIBUTES

There are several ways of defining customers - by age, sex, education - or perhaps by what stage they are at in the family life cycle (single, young married couple, etc.).

The second way of analysing market segments is through *customer attributes*. The great advantage of knowing what your customers are actually like is that you can *communicate* with them.

Or the definition could be based on socio-economic groupings.

Such grouping are useful when it comes to, say, advertising. One section of your customers is reached via newspapers like 'The Times', others by *The Sun*. Poster and TV advertisements can be angled at one section or another.

Demographic and socio-economic groupings allow you to assess the best way of communicating with your customers.

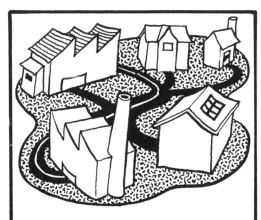

Demographic segmetation in industrial markets enables customers to be classified by size, production processes, markets served, industry type, geographical location, numbers of employees, and so on.

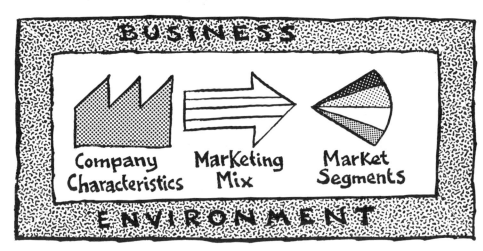

In our map of the business, the marketing model, we have now completed the customer audit, and explained what is meant by the term 'market segmentation'.

In the next chapter we will look at the *marketing mix,* in particular the part concerned with what we sell - the product.

Summary of Chapter 4

The first stage in planning and implementing an effective marketing strategy is to define in precise and actionable terms just who the organization's customers are or could be. Knowing where sales are coming from, and the source of profits, is the key to understanding current market positions and to assessing the potential for the future. A number of questions immediately present themselves. For example, are the customer and the consumer the same? What measures can be used to define a market?

Recognizing that customers differ from each other in terms of who they are and why they buy provides opportunities for market segmentation. The means by which groups of customers are distinguished from each other is important and attention has to be paid to the choice of criteria for segmentation. Customers can be categorized on many dimensions, but only those criteria which relate in some way to purchasing behaviour and which are themselves actionable are of any use to the strategist.

We need to understand that markets are made up of people and we need to discover how these people can be grouped together into a number of sub-markets or market segments, for example, by referring to the way they buy (frequently, in bulk, cheaper products, once a year etc) or to the benefits they seek (quality, service, status, cost savings etc).

REMEMBER:
Know your Customer
Know your Strengths
Sell Benefits.

Chapter 5
The Product Audit

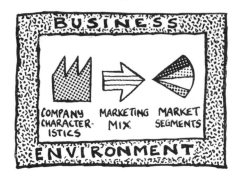

In the last chapter we saw how an audit of the business's customers can give us an understanding of what we mean by market segments.

In this chapter we're going to concentrate on one of the elements of the marketing mix.

We'll see how we measure the products or services offered by a company. But first, let's ask a fundamental question: What is a product?

Take this product

A quarter-inch bit. But when people buy it, is *this* really what they want? Or is it this?

When it becomes cheaper to make quarter-inch holes by other means, the company making bits will have to go over to the new method to stay in business.

This is because people buy *benefits*, not *products*. Remember this?:

WHICH MEANS THAT

Products are only bought if they bring the benefits that customers want. As we saw in the last chapter, benefits are related to things other than technical performance.

Take the case of the man who wanted to buy a car.

He saw his purchase in terms of getting from A to B (a *rational* consideration), but he also saw it in terms of his image (an emotional consideration). It's because customers' needs are not always entirely rational that a company's product decisions should not be left only to the Research and Development Department or to engineers.

Here's another very important characteristic of products - and it applies to services too:

NOTHING OFFERS BENEFITS WHICH LAST FOR EVER

All products have *life cycles*.

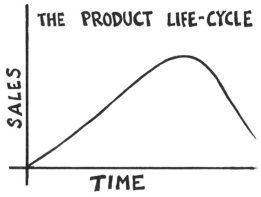

THE PRODUCT LIFE-CYCLE

SALES

TIME

The sales performance of any product rises from nothing when the product is introduced to the market, reaches a peak and then declines to nothing again. We can illustrate the reasons for this by taking the case of a company which had unsuccessfully tried to market children's toy cowboy hats made out of injection moulded plastic.

A mistake in the process had made them mis-shapen and unsaleable.

In throwing away one of the offending products the managing director made an interesting discovery.

Try as he might, he could not get rid of the hat.

Everytime he threw it, it returned to him in a perfect arc. As a hat it was a failure, but as a boomerang it was an outstanding success.

As soon as they could think of a suitable name, the product was marketed.

It was instantly successful and, in a few short months, there was a huge growth in sales.

At this point competition appeared. Other firms were quick to cash in on the success of the Frizbang and produce their own versions.

The product caught on. Nearly everyone was buying it, and it seemed that nearly everyone was selling it too. But after a while the craze began to wear off. The growth rate slowed. There were fewer customers and too many suppliers.

A price war started, and firms which were not prepared for this began to drop out. Finally the craze itself disappeared and, as the saying goes, the product became old hat.

It went the way of the hula hoop, and those companies which had no other product to offer went out of business. Here we've seen an example of a product life cycle.

It went through five stages. Sales grow slowly at the introduction stage when the product is new on the market and few people know of it. Then sales increase rapidly during the growth phase. It is now that competitors enter the market and promote their own products. Sooner or later the rate of growth slows. This is the maturity period; and then the market gets saturated because there are too many firms competing for customers. A price war starts and some companies drop out. The market finally declines and the product in its existing form becomes unprofitable.

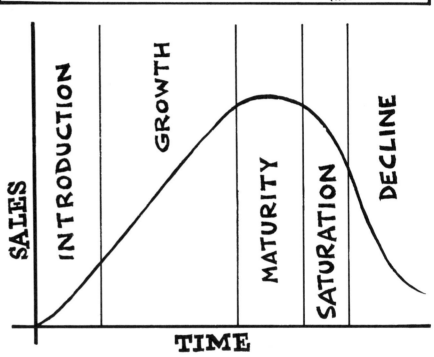

This is what happens when the company marketing the product takes no corrective action. However, the life cycle of a product can be prolonged.

If, just before the saturation phase the product *range* is extended, there could be a new period of growth on the curve.

And, when that begins to drop off, a new market could be developed for the product, so keeping the life cycle going for longer still. One part of the life cycle is still missing. It comes at the beginning.

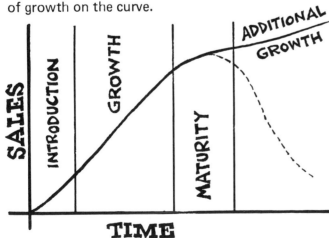

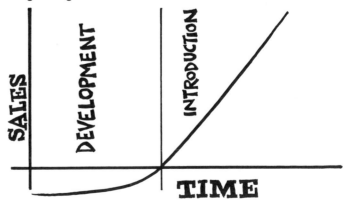

32

The development phase of a product life cycle is expensive because it does not bring in sales and is therefore a net loss; but it is essential to the existence of the product however long or short its life cycle. So, taking all the various elements into consideration, a life cycle of a product could look like this:

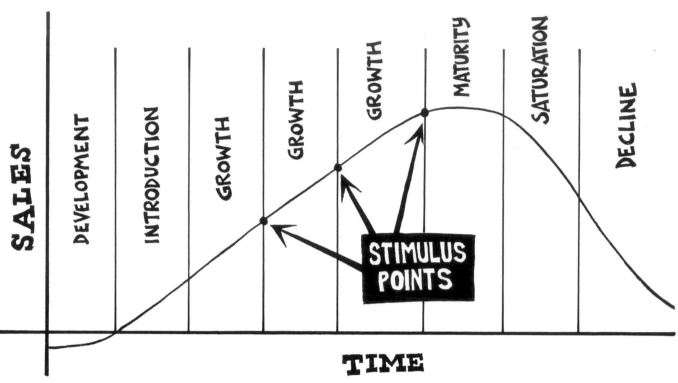

First, there's the initial development period, the introduction of the product to the market and then a succession of periods of growth stimulated in various ways: product improvement, an extension of the product range, market development, etc. These prolong the life cycle before it goes through the inevitable phases of maturity, saturation and decline.

The Product Life-Cycle affects the Marketing Mix

Each of the four elements of the mix responds in its own way - for instance, we've seen that the *product* itself might have to change during its life; and if the company gets involved in a price war its *pricing* policy will have to be flexible or it will lose its market share - a crucial factor when the market declines. The *place* could change radically between the introductory phase and the end of the growth phase. The same goes for *promotion*, since during the introductory phase it is important to create awareness of the existence of the product whereas during the growth phase it might be necessary to point out the advantages of the company's product over its competitors'.

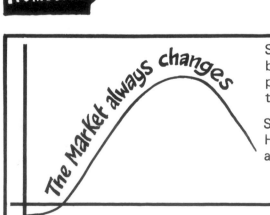

So the product life cycle is important to all areas of the company because it creates awareness of the constant change that is taking place with every product. What will be a successful policy at one time is unlikely to be so at another.

So far, we've discussed one product and its life cycle in isolation. However, most firms sell more than one product or product range at a time.

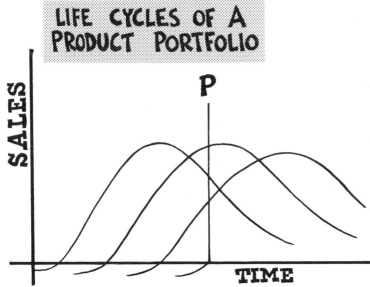

LIFE CYCLES OF A PRODUCT PORTFOLIO

Each will have its own life cycle, different in duration, each starting at a different time. Not all of them will be of equal importance. This collection of products is known as a PRODUCT PORTFOLIO. The line P represents a particular date in this company's history. One product is in decline, one at saturation and one is just about to be introduced to the market place. Now, if it is to grow profitably over a long period, the company should aim to achieve continuous growth by introducing products in a well-timed way. This is the principle behind the management of a portfolio of products.

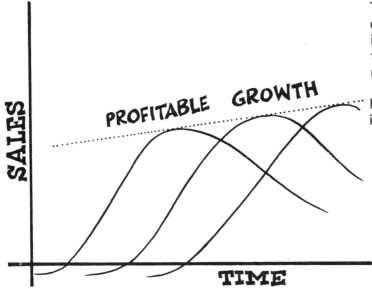

The idea of a portfolio is to balance growth, cash flow and risk. As markets grow or shrink, individual products will progress or decline and the product portfolio will change, so it is necessary to review the portfolio regularly.

Knowledge of the product life cycle is important in our understanding of marketing management.

The next key concept we'll look at is the relationship between *market share* and *market growth*. First let's be clear about what they are and begin by examining the importance of market share.

These two products are competing for the same market. In performance they are virtually identical and they are the same price. But the makers of product B have an advantage over the makers of product A.

This is because B costs less to produce than A.

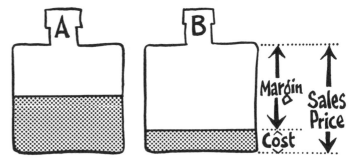

So B's margin of profit is greater than A's, because it can practice economies of scale since it sells more. In other words, it has a *larger market share* than A.

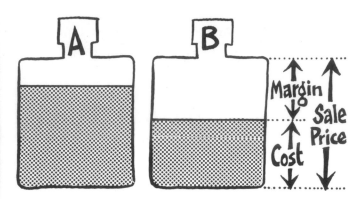

When, during the maturity phase, price cutting starts, the percentage of cost to the sales price goes up in both cases, so the margins for both A and B come down.

But now, B's margin though reduced is proportionally much bigger than A's, and A will feel the effects of the price war more severely than B.

So a *large market share* is a desirable goal, regardless of the size of the market. But we have to be clear about what the word 'market' means.

e.g.

This relatively small company supplies industrial bearings - in theory a huge market, so a casual observer might think that this company has a very small market share. But in practice the company commands a very large share of what turns out to be a highly specialised market; so it's in just as strong a position as a much bigger company offering a more generalised product. So a high market share is necessary for success irrespective of the size of the market.

We've now looked at *market share*. What about *market growth*?

In markets which grow slowly (which might include frictionles marine bearings) it would be costly and difficult for a company to increase its market share. The market is probably mature, with the product life cycle reaching saturation point, and it may be dominated by a few relatively major firms.

But in markets which grow quickly it's a different story, because if a company tries to get the biggest share possible very quickly, it is costly in promotional terms. So many companies make the mistake of sitting tight since they seem to be doing well in an expanding market, but they will have *growth rates lower than the growth rate of the market*. This gradually gives a cost advantage to more aggressive competitors, as we saw with firms A and B above.

These ideas relating to market share and market growth have been combined into a matrix by the Boston Consulting Group.

Market Growth ↑

THE BOSTON MATRIX

Market Share →

The matrix reflects a given company's *relative* share and growth in any market.

← —— **TOTAL MARKET** —— →

For example, suppose this area represents the total market for a certain product, and also suppose that firms C and D are competitors in this market.

10% 20% 30% 40% 50% 60% 70% 80% 90% 100%

C | D

← —— **TOTAL MARKET** —— →

In this case, D, the biggest firm in the market has twice C's market share, although in absolute terms the difference in their share is only 10% of the whole market.

The *market share* axis of the matrix is the *measure of dominance* of the company relative to its biggest competitor in the market. So D is twice as dominant as C since it has twice the share of the market, or a ratio of 2:1. And conversely the ratio of C to D is 0.5 or 1:2.

The *market growth* axis measures the average annual growth rate of all the markets in which a firm sells its goods or services.

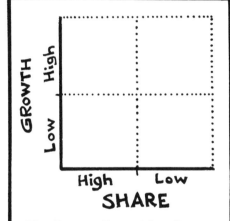

GROWTH — High / Low
SHARE — High / Low

The Boston Consulting Group has divided each axis into two, thus providing a graph with four areas, or quadrants.

These four quadrants are:
high growth with high market share;
high growth, low share;
low growth, high share;
and low growth, low share.

The sales performance of any company's products will earn them a place in one of these quadrants.

GROWTH — High / Low

| Star | Wildcat |
| Cash Cow | Dog |

SHARE — High / Low

The Boston Group has labelled these areas appropriately - and each label gives an idea of the cash-earning prospects of products in each quadrant.

So a *star* product has achieved a high market share and generates lots of cash, but because the market is growing rapidly the company probably also uses lots of cash to maintain its dominant market position.

A wildcat (or question mark) is one which has not yet attained a dominant market position, or perhaps did so once but has now slipped. The market is growing rapidly and if the company wishes to gain market share in order to get the reward of a better relative cost position it will have to make a quite heavy cash investment.

A cash cow, on the other hand, is a leader in a market where there is little market growth - i.e. in a mature market. Cash cows are excellent generators of cash and need little to keep them going because of the state of the market. They are the most profitable source of income for any company.

Finally, dogs have very little future and are often a cash drain on the company because there is little or no market growth and because competitors' costs are much lower. Spending money on them is probably a waste of time and they frequently owe their existence to managerial ego rather than business sense. They are candidates for divestment unless, of course, they are there as an essential part of a product range in order to support other products.

So we can summarise the net cash situation for an entire product portfolio like this:

Star	Wildcat
O	—
Cash Cow	Dog
+	O

Stars are just about self-financing, so represent zero cash generation; wildcats have not yet become profitable, so they represent net cash outflow. Cash cows mean profit for the business, while dogs are generally ignored but don't make money either, so they do not represent either profit or loss.

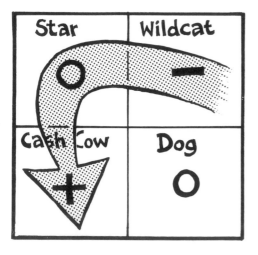

Products move from wildcats to stars, from which they mature into cash cows, where they will be the next source of finance for the next generation of stars and selected wildcats.

This is how the Boston matrix can be used to cover a whole range or portfolio of products. It can also illustrate a company's forecast of the future market position of a product, given that the company's policies remain unchanged over the period.

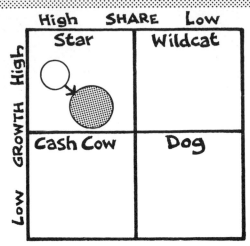

The white circle represents a product. Its position shows its relative share and growth, and the size of the circle represents the contribution of the product to the company's sales volume. The forecast of this product is shown by the shaded circle. This represents how the company thinks it will be doing in five years' time. Here the position of the shaded circle shows that the company forecasts a drop both in market share and in the rate of market growth. Also its larger size could mean that the product is likely to represent a larger share of the company's revenue. This forecast could well mean bad news unless the other products in the portfolio compensate for it so that the company's future is secure.

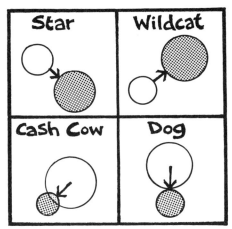

However, as you can see, the wildcat as well as the star has lost market share, the cash cow has moved slightly towards a bigger share - but market growth is slowing down even further - and the dog has all but disappeared. If this is the forecast position in say, three years' time, the chances are that the company still will be profitable. But all the danger signs are there. The star and the wildcat are heading towards the dog box when the life cycle effect slows the market growth rate down. And when this happens the company will only have dogs and may well go out of business.

So, the Boston matrix is particularly useful for predicting the fortunes of a company, and when used in conjunction with the product life cycle, it can help us make decisions about each main product in the range. But its assumptions are based only upon market share and market growth, and some companies need a more flexible version of the matrix, since market share for certain kinds of products may well have little to do with profitability, as for example in the case of products that share the same basic production processes. The main thing to remember is that a company should define its markets in such a way that it enables it to be competitive. To help with this, companies like General Electric, McKinsey and Shell have widened the ideas behind the Boston grid.

Summary of Chapter 5

The strategy which an organization adopts towards its product is the most important factor in determining its long term success. Continued successful performance, however, depends on the ability of organizations to base their product offering on a dynamic view of the marketplace. They must recognize that the marketing environment will change over time and will demand a changed response from them, typically in the form of a programme of adjustment to their product-market strategy.

Products make profits for the company by effectively providing customers with the benefits they seek within carefully controlled cost and revenue parameters. The concept of the product life cycle is a particularly useful tool for marketers, who can use it along with their carefully acquired knowledge of their particular markets to assess whether a product is in a stage of growth, maturity or decline. They can then go on to develop appropriate marketing strategies.

Decisions on product-market strategy must be made in the context of a product range portfolio which should maintain a suitable balance of growth products, mature products and declining products. Only if such a portfolio is built up in a balanced way will the organization have a sound base on which to plan for future development, particularly the development of new products.

REMEMBER:
The two key marketing factors about the product audit...

GROWTH

SHARE

Star Wildcat Cash Cow Dog

Chapter 6
Setting Marketing Objectives & Strategies

In this chapter we're going to concentrate on a key step in the marketing planning process, the step in which all the information accumulated in the product, customer and market audits will be used. It is the fourth stage in the marketing planning process ...

... the formulation of marketing objectives and strategies.

To find out what these are we'll go back to the business jungle, where one tribe is doing quite well.

They had discovered that if they collected a useless metal called gold which lay all over the place they could trade it with gullible tourists for useful things like old paper bags and surplus army blankets.

Their leader was a wise old man who, though quite small, was extremely far sighted.

In fact, the reason the tribe did better than all the others in the jungle was that the leader could see further and therefore make wiser decisions than anyone else. He had some magic words to describe this. He called his decisions 'corporate objectives'.

Though none of the tribe quite knew what this meant they did know that he relied on their support for his wisdom; and *they* relied upon *his* decision to make *their* decisions. Like this

THERE'S MORE GOLD LADS! WE'LL CROSS THAT RIVER!

RIGHT! THAT MEANS A BRIDGE!

OK! I'LL GET THE LADS COLLECTING WOOD!

So any decision the leader made affected everyone else's decisions - and conversely, the old man's corporate decisions were based on his knowledge of what the people under him could do.

Corporate objectives will define what the business as a whole wants to achieve, and this is usually expressed in financial terms. They will suggest strategies, or ways and means of achieving other objectives lower down the business hierarchy, so that the business will have a common purpose. The activities of a neighbouring tribe illustrate this.

They all had their own ideas about how to succeed in business. They never told each other anything, went off in all directions and never achieved anything.

On the other hand the smart tribe were aware of the strength their co-ordinated action gave them; so they were able to plan, from broad objectives to specific ones, for example

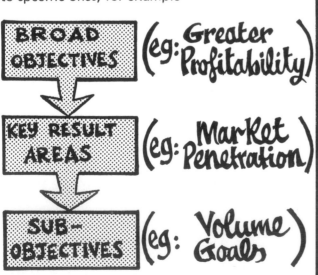

Decisions taken at any level, if they take no account of possible effects anywhere else in the organisation, may have a short-term benefit but could compromise other more long-term plans. In fact the further down the hierarchical chain one goes, the more important it is that objectives at that level derive from objectives at a higher level.

I'M GOING TO LEAD A MORE MEANINGFUL LIFE.... TOMORROW.

CHARACTERISTICS OF OBJECTIVES

* MEASURABLE ATTRIBUTE
* YARDSTICK
* ATTAINABLE POINT

An objective is not a vague aim, however worthwhile. It must have three sets of criteria by which it is assessed.

The first characteristic is the *measurable attribute* of the objective, the way in which it is normally quantified, e.g. by number, weight or volume. Car sales are measured in units, petrol sales by litres. The *yardstick* defines, e.g. the number of sales possible in any given market, while the *attainable point* on the scale defines the percentage of sales which the company could expect to make.

Marketing objectives are generally stated in quantitative terms

MARKETING OBJECTIVES

Standards of performance — These might relate to sales performance measured in sales volume. The attribute would be the measure of profitability

Conditions which have to be achieved — These could be measured in terms of the percentage of market share or outlet penetration

How do we *set* marketing objectives?

BOSTON MATRIX

MARKET GROWTH

| Star | Wildcat |
| Cash Cow | Dog |

MARKET SHARE

Products will fall into one or more of these categories, therefore the marketing decisions affecting them are likely to change.

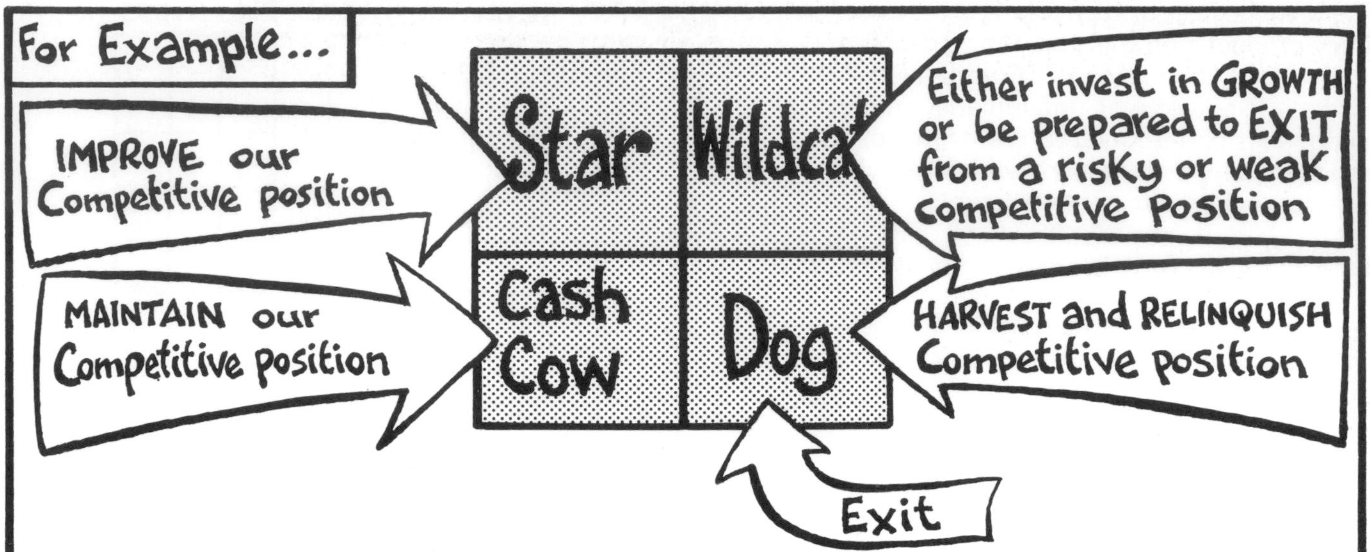
For Example...
Star
Wildcat
Cash Cow
Dog
IMPROVE our Competitive position
MAINTAIN our Competitive position
Either invest in GROWTH or be prepared to EXIT from a risky or weak competitive position
HARVEST and RELINQUISH Competitive position
Exit

In each quadrant - with each kind of product - the appropriate marketing response is likely to be different from the others.

REMEMBER, MARKETING IS ABOUT TWO THINGS: PRODUCTS & MARKETS

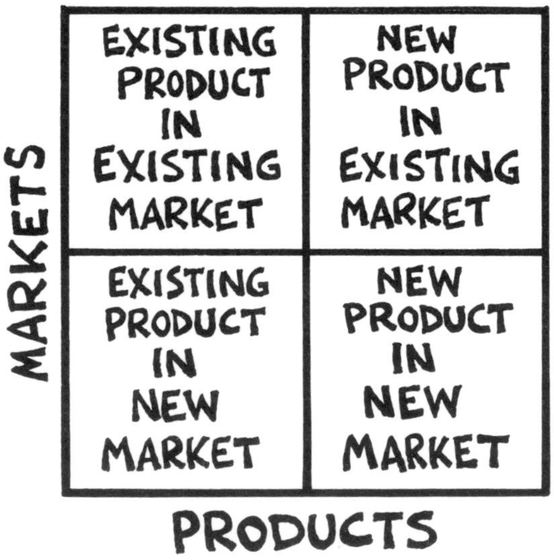
EXISTING PRODUCT IN EXISTING MARKET
NEW PRODUCT IN EXISTING MARKET
EXISTING PRODUCT IN NEW MARKET
NEW PRODUCT IN NEW MARKET
MARKETS
PRODUCTS

ANSOFF'S MATRIX

This permutation of products and markets is called Ansoff's Matrix. The term 'new products' means technical innovation and 'new markets' refers to changing markets. It's important to realise that there will be different marketing responses to each permutation in the Matrix.

In the same way, when we get back to Ansoff's Matrix of the relationship between products and markets, we must respond differently to different permutations.

Formulation of marketing objectives for each quadrant of the Ansoff Matrix will be different for different companies because each business will have its own strengths and weaknesses, and each will be affected differently by the opportunities and threats of the outside environment. What's more, this diagram is a simplification of the marketplace, which is never as clear cut as the four boxes in this Matrix suggests.

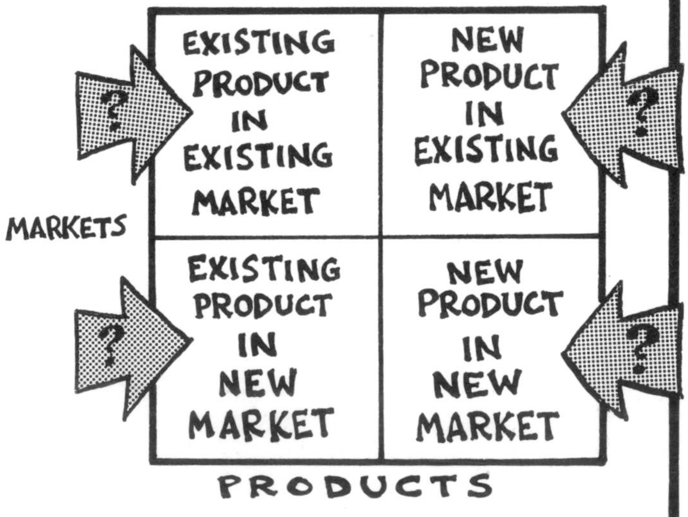
EXISTING PRODUCT IN EXISTING MARKET
NEW PRODUCT IN EXISTING MARKET
EXISTING PRODUCT IN NEW MARKET
NEW PRODUCT IN NEW MARKET
MARKETS
PRODUCTS
?
?
?
?

There are degrees of technological 'newness' in every product, and there are many shades of familiar and unfamiliar situations in every market. The degree of unfamiliarity in either component corresponds to the degree of risk entertained by the company which ventures into either new products *or* new markets.

But as products go through their life cycles, and as markets expand or contract, companies will be forced into riskier situations in their search for sales and profits.

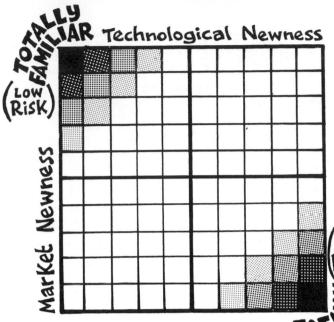

The systematic way of coping with this change is through the SWOT Analysis

The SWOT Analysis, the third step in the marketing planning process, is an analysis of the company's strengths and weaknesses and the opportunities and threats presented by the business environment. The SWOT Analysis is based on the marketing audit and leads to the formulation of marketing objectives and strategies.

In this way, development will be based as far as possible on the company's strengths and will take maximum advantage of external opportunities. If this is not done, whatever technical developments the company makes are likely to prove unsuccessful in the long run.

The mechanics of the fourth step involve, first of all, the setting of marketing objectives. This depends, as we've seen, on the relationship between existing or new products and markets. Then, because these objectives have to be measurable, we must identify the criteria for determining whether or not the objectives have been reached (remember the three attributes of objectives?) Finally, from the SWOT Analysis the opportunities and threats of the market place are identified, and from this the final marketing plan can be prepared.

WHAT ARE MARKETING STRATEGIES?

If an objective is *'What we want'*, then a strategy is *'How we get it'*. However, a strategy is not concerned with detail. It does *not* delineate individual courses of action. It will contain three elements

THE MEANS
THE TIMETABLE
THE RESOURCES

Which means that it will define broadly the means of implementing a marketing plan. It will include the timing of the programme, and it will call for the necessary resources for the job as and when certain actions have to be taken.

The marketing strategy is like a military action in that it is concerned with the overall plan for a particular target - or market, and the four elements of the marketing mix are the ingredients of the plan - different variations in each ingredient for different markets.

So far we have considered a situation where corporate objectives, audits, sales forecasts and the resultant SWOT Analysis have been in perfect harmony, resulting in marketing objectives which have been easy to identify.

But what about this?

The Sales Director makes a forecast, only to discover that it is *not good enough!*

45

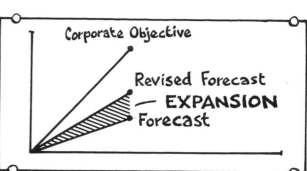

The Corporate Objective demands *more*. There is a gap between Corporate Objective and sales forecast. What is to be done?

Well, the gap can be partly filled by a *revised forecast* which will rely on expansion - on increased productivity, or perhaps improved market penetration. This might be arrived at by reducing costs, increasing prices, improving the marketing mix, planning for a bigger share of the market, and so on. But what about the rest of the gap? You may have to consider developing new products for your existing markets, finding new markets for your existing products, or some combination of both of these.

	EXISTING PRODUCT	NEW PRODUCT
MARKETS	EXISTING PRODUCT IN EXISTING MARKET →	NEW PRODUCT IN EXISTING MARKET
	EXISTING PRODUCT IN NEW MARKET	NEW PRODUCT IN NEW MARKET

PRODUCTS

Under the circumstances it might pay to move horizontally along the product line, because it takes years to build a reputation in new markets - and a company's reputation in one market is not easily transferred to another. A competent marketing audit should ensure that the method chosen is consistent with the company's strengths. For instance, the development of new products should reflect this consistency.

FIRST WE BROUGHT YOU

THEN WE CAME UP WITH

AND AFTER THAT WE GAVE YOU

...NOW WE PROUDLY PRESENT PLASTIC GLU NEW!

Here the product can be sold through existing channels using the same sales force.

But what if the China glue company had done this?

USE **OUR** GLU© ON **OUR** CHINA

Marketing china cups and saucers to people who use their glue will have implications for production, distribution, sales force and technical development. However, product extension *can* be one way of filling the gap.

The employment of product extension is a *new strategy*. Another could be market extension or diversification; but the techniques of expansion and new strategies both have their own problems.

Measures to improve productivity in order to expand must be realistic - and your determination to reduce marketing costs may not be possible in some markets or for some products. On the other hand, market penetration might pay off if it involves existing products and markets, because it is the least costly or risky.

TOTALLY FAMILIAR

(LOW RISK)

EXISTING PRODUCTS IN EXISTING MARKETS	NEW PRODUCTS IN EXISTING MARKETS
EXISTING PRODUCTS IN NEW MARKETS	NEW PRODUCTS IN NEW MARKETS

(HIGH RISK)

TOTALLY UNFAMILIAR

As we saw earlier, it is riskiest of all to go into new markets with new products. These few points indicate some of the problems of implementing new strategies or attempting to expand your existing markets or product range.

Finally, it is obvious that marketing objectives and strategies are intimately connected; but remember that they must also be linked to the overall objectives of the company.

Corporate Objectives lead to corporate strategies, which in turn suggest objectives lower down the scale.

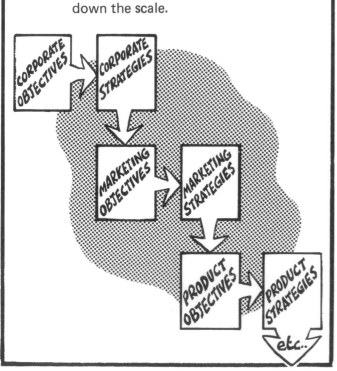

At the same time there are different but related hierarchies within other divisions of the organisation.

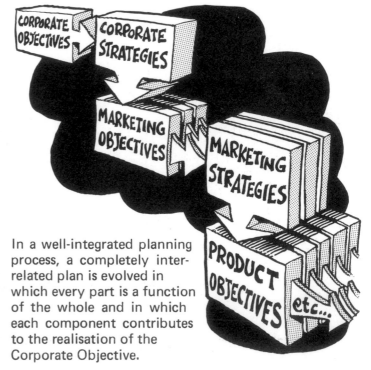

In a well-integrated planning process, a completely inter-related plan is evolved in which every part is a function of the whole and in which each component contributes to the realisation of the Corporate Objective.

Summary of Chapter 6

Setting marketing objectives and the attendant strategies to achieve them is undoubtedly the key step in the marketing planning process.

Corporate objectives are generally concerned with measurements relating to the long run profitability of the organization, such as return on investment, profit before tax, earnings per share, and so on. The strategies to achieve these objectives, such as whether to manufacture or buy in, to do one's own distribution or to get outside contractors to do it, how to manage cash flow, the size and character of the labour force, and of course what products to offer and which markets to trade in, are all examples of corporate strategies.

The latter, however, at the functional level of marketing, ie what to sell and who to sell it to, are examples of marketing objectives, which are concerned with one or more of the following: existing products in existing markets; new products in existing markets; existing products in new markets; and new products in new markets. The latter is, of course, the riskiest route to take, because it takes an organization furthest away from its distinctive competence. All of these objectives must be measurable, in terms such as volume, value, market share, outlet penetration, profit and so on.

Marketing strategies can be likened to a military action, in that they are concerned with the overall means of achieving an objective. The four elements of the marketing mix - product, price, promotion and place are the ingredients of the plan. These will be different for different markets.

REMEMBER: Plan from broad Objectives...

...to specific ones, through Key result areas...

...to sub-objectives

OBJECTIVES SUGGEST STRATEGIES

Chapter 7
The Communication Plan: I
The Advertising & Sales Promotion Plans

In earlier chapters we've seen that we first set marketing objectives, and from these we can devise the appropriate strategies to meet the objectives.

In plainer language we mean this. 'How to do it' is related to the marketing mix, through its four elements.

In this chapter and the next we concentrate on the element of *promotion* - on the business of communicating with customers.

Businesses communicate with their customers in a wide variety of ways, but there are two main categories, *impersonal* and *personal* communications.

Impersonal communications are things like advertising, point-of-sale displays, promotions, PR and so on . . .

While personal communications mean direct face-to-face meetings, for example between a salesman and his customer. In the first of these two chapters on communication we'll deal with impersonal communications, and in the second we'll look at the importance of personal communications.

The first thing to do is to decide on the communications mix - in other words, the split between personal and impersonal communication.

How can we decide? Let's assume we want to sell capital goods to the confectionery industry.

Yummo employs about 300 people, but we won't have to address ourselves to every one of them. On the other hand, we shouldn't make the mistake of thinking that any one person can unlock the doors either. In a firm that size we'll have to convince about five people, and they'll all need different arguments.

WHICH MEANS THAT....

TOFFEE NEWS

And whereas some will be pleased to see salesmen, others will be more influenced by trade and technical publications in their choice of products. So, each individual members of the client company's decision-making group could require a different approach.

Their different perceptions result from the different ways they see the firm.

For instance, suppose Yummo wanted to buy a new toffee-wrapping machine, what steps would it take before a brand-new machine was installed?

First, it recognises it has a problem. In this case it can't solve it alone. A specialist toffee-wrapping supplier must be found.

YUMMO RESEARCH

The characteristics and quality of what's needed are worked out - in other words, the specifications for solving the problem are defined and drawn up.

YELLOW PAGES

GAMMA MACHINES

TOFFEE TECH

ACME

BETA WRAPPERS

catalogue

A search is made for possible suppliers, either for the supply of special components or for complete items of plant.

Potential suppliers submit tenders and ultimately one is selected. An order is placed . . .

A B C

and in the fullness of time

YUMMO

DELTA

the new equipment is delivered. In *this* case there was a new process involving new circumstances, so a number of people were involved in the decision-making process.

So any supplier or salesman faced with a situation like this will have to satisfy quite a large number of people over a fairly long period, answering a wide range of queries and building a commitment from individuals with markedly different viewpoints to buy his products. Because a salesman couldn't possibly do all this there exists a need for *indirect* communication.

A major vehicle of indirect communication is advertising, about which there has long been a common misconception.

This is that there's a simple cause-and-effect link between advertising and sales. The facts reveal it is more complex.

First comes the dawning of awareness, the recognition of the existence of a product.

Then comes comprehension and the comfortable belief in the purpose of the product. Then . . .

The conviction that a certain product offers certain benefits. And finally . . .

. . . The *action* - the decision to buy the product. So, advertising is not the straightforward activity that some believe it to be. There is no *direct* relationship between advertising and sales. Other factors - product quality, prices, service levels and so on play an important part in sales success. Nevertheless, if we are going to advertise, we should know *what* we are trying to achieve. We need to set objectives.

ADVERTISING OBJECTIVES MUST BE MEASURABLE

And they must be attainable. For instance:

It's no good making claims for your product if those claims can be disproved.

Equally, it's no good making irrelevant claims.

So the first thing to do in setting advertising objectives is to decide on what reasonable objectives there are.

This is a respectable objective for advertising, but only if the objective can be achieved by advertising *alone*. Advertising objectives are not only related to customer awareness or product information.

They can be concerned with changing attitudes, creating desires, giving reassurance, and so on. It is for the company concerned to set its own advertising objectives which will also be affected by the identity of the target audience, the character of the market segment, market share, budget, timing and other factors . . .

. . . like the position in the life cycle of the product.

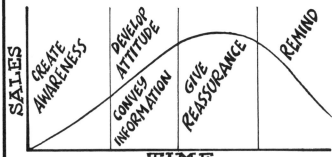

For instance, advertising objectives may change like this throughout the product's life cycle; but there is another factor which has a profound effect on the chain of advertising objectives: diffusion of innovation.

This means that not everyone is equally prepared to accept new products or ideas at the same time - and in terms of advertising the approach made to people who are eager to try new things will be essentially different from the approach made to more conservative consumers.

The first people to adopt new products we call innovators and they make up a very small part of the eventual market.

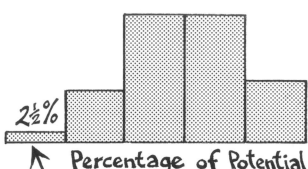

2½%

Percentage of Potential
Adopters over time

↑

INNOVATORS

So when a product or service is first introduced it will in general be taken up by those people who like to try new things out, and experience has shown this to be about 2½% of any market. But as the product gets more well known, more people buy it.

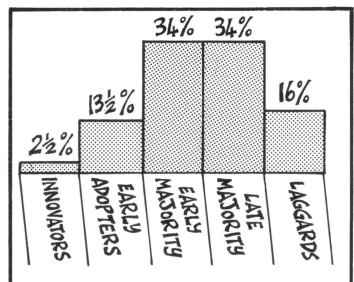

34% 34%

13½%

16%

2½%

INNOVATORS | EARLY ADOPTERS | EARLY MAJORITY | LATE MAJORITY | LAGGARDS

People with status adopt the product early, making it acceptable and respectable so that its success is more or less guaranteed. The early majority start buying - these are the more conservative customers; they in turn are followed by the more sceptical late majority, and lastly come the laggards whose low income and status in society make them eternally followers rather than leaders. This pattern demonstrates the need for different kinds of advertising for each category of customer, and this again points to the need to consider a different set of advertising objectives for different stages in a product's life cycle.

The Taste of the NEW!
YUMMO
For the Few who KNOW

YEAH,.... COOL!

At first the target might be the innovative customer, and once sales have passed the 3% mark the target might change to the early adopters.

KEEP AHEAD OF THE JONESES

BUT OF COURSE DARLING

EAT YUM!

And when 10-12% of the possible market is buying the product, the advertising strategy might change from the presentation of a new product to a widely accepted one.

FIT YOUR ADVERTISING STRATEGY TO THE CHARACTERISTICS OF EACH CUSTOMER GROUP

Advertising affects people other than consumers. It can be directed at suppliers, at channels of distribution, shareholders, employers, government - in fact anyone who has an influence on the company's success.

Having decided on *what* we want to say and *whom* we want to say it to, the strategy, timing and costs, can now be decided. The strategy might include the advertising media used, the tone of the campaign, frequency, and who does what and when.

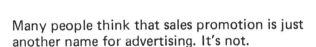

Many people think that sales promotion is just another name for advertising. It's not.

Advertising does things like describing some characteristic of the product, or explaining some benefit. Whereas, sales promotion . . .

. . . makes an offer of a feature, usually to defined customers, within a specific time limit. In other words, to qualify as a sales promotion, someone must be offered something which is featured, rather than just being an aspect of trade. Furthermore, the offer must include benefits not inherent in the product or service, as opposed to the intangible benefits offered in advertising, such as adding value through appeals to imagery. So, how does a company *use* sales promotion?

Well, it's a very useful device for persuading customers to bring forward their decision to buy. In this case it's an attempt to diffuse the high demand for cars in August. This will help the manufacturer's *distribution problem* rather than sell cars. Other sales promotion activities include the encouragement of repeat purchases, counter-action of competitors, appeals to marginal buys, getting bills paid early, etc.

There are many types of sales promotion. Here, extra products are offered - and this is subtly different from a straight cut-price offer in that the customer is being encouraged to stock-pile the product, so increasing his brand-loyalty. On the other hand it may not work with a customer who is after a short-term bargain; so sales promotion has to be used with care, and again the type of customer being appealed to must be borne in mind.

Some forms of sales promotion have become permanent features of a company's activity (like Co-op stamps) but, by and large, most companies regard it as a tactical device to be used at intervals, yielding spasmodic results. This contrasts with the notion of advertising as a strategic, long-term activity which changes with the product life cycle. But some companies have managed to incorporate long-term sales promotion campaigns into their advertising strategies - so though difficult, it's

not impossible. Because of this very difficulty, care must be taken in drawing up a sales promotion plan. Obviously, the budgeting of such a plan should ensure that the company does not end up *losing* money if the plan is *successful*; so the first essential step is to establish a sales promotion *objective*, in the same way as the company sets *advertising* or *distribution* objectives. Each promotion might have different objectives, such as trial, a shift in buying peaks, combating competition and so on.

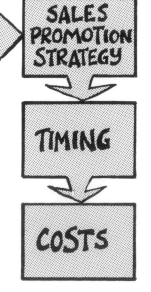

And then, the strategy to implement the objective must be worked out. The appropriate sales promotion technique must be selected and pre-tested. The promotion campaign must then be mounted and finally evaluated in depth. Spending must be analysed and categorised (e.g. whether the money has gone on special packaging, on point of sale material, or price reductions, and so on).

So in producing a sales promotion plan, once again the planner goes through the familiar process of setting *sales promotion objectives* which will be dependent upon the company's *marketing objectives*. These might include stock control, distribution, manipulation of customer buyer patterns and so on. The sales promotion *strategy* follows from this, with its selection of the appropriate techniques and media, and finally the timescale and costings must be controlled with great care.

Summary of Chapter 7

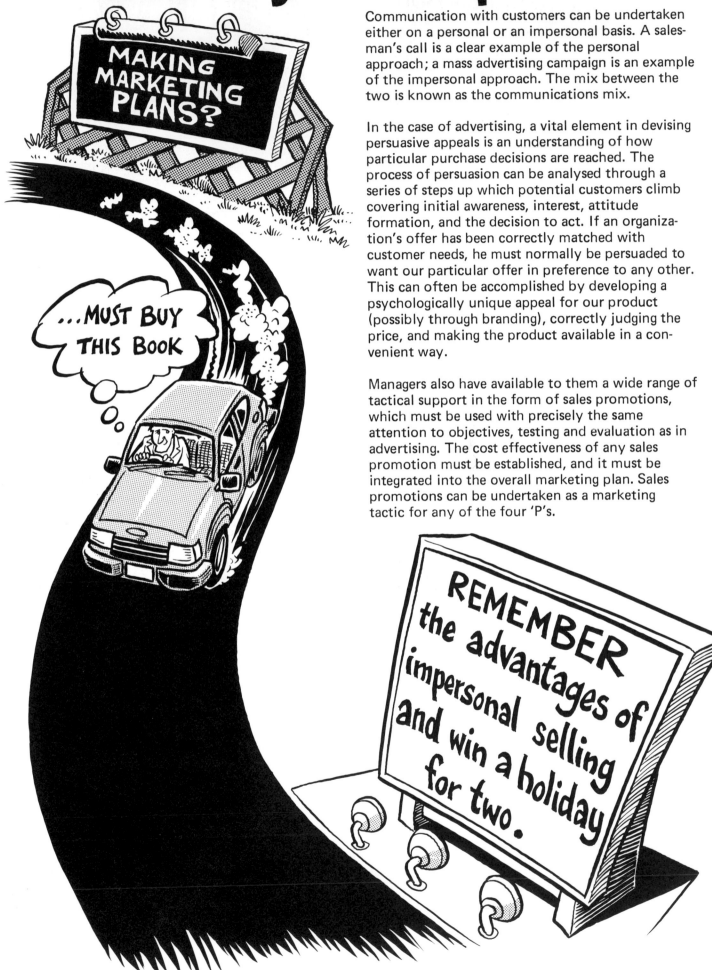

Communication with customers can be undertaken either on a personal or an impersonal basis. A salesman's call is a clear example of the personal approach; a mass advertising campaign is an example of the impersonal approach. The mix between the two is known as the communications mix.

In the case of advertising, a vital element in devising persuasive appeals is an understanding of how particular purchase decisions are reached. The process of persuasion can be analysed through a series of steps up which potential customers climb covering initial awareness, interest, attitude formation, and the decision to act. If an organization's offer has been correctly matched with customer needs, he must normally be persuaded to want our particular offer in preference to any other. This can often be accomplished by developing a psychologically unique appeal for our product (possibly through branding), correctly judging the price, and making the product available in a convenient way.

Managers also have available to them a wide range of tactical support in the form of sales promotions, which must be used with precisely the same attention to objectives, testing and evaluation as in advertising. The cost effectiveness of any sales promotion must be established, and it must be integrated into the overall marketing plan. Sales promotions can be undertaken as a marketing tactic for any of the four 'P's.

Chapter 8
The Communication Plan:II
The Sales Plan

In this chapter we turn to the second part of the Communications Plan. We're going to look at *personal* selling - how important is it? How many salesmen does a company need? What should they do? How does personal selling work?

Sales representatives are central to most commercial activities, so it's surprising that sales management is such a neglected area of marketing management. Other considerations often seem to come first, considerations linked to other aspects of the business.

This is because few marketing or production managers have actually been salesmen themselves so they misunderstand the salesman's role in the marketing mix and under-estimate the importance of efficient salesmanship. What's more, salesmen themselves contribute to this neglect.

Salesmen see themselves as being at the 'sharp end' - face to face with the customer, without the protective barricade of office, factory, bar-charts and theoretical mumbo-jumbo to hide behind.

Of course, such reasoning is misleading . . .

. . . because a great deal of marketing planning must take place *before* any effort by the sales force is made . . .

. . . so that when the salesman enters the marketplace he has a better chance of making a successful sale. Also the distinction between theory and practice becomes even less when we recognise the existence of market segments and product-portfolios - marketing planning concepts which are hard and useful facts to the salesman. And there's the problem of *change*.

New customers and markets may well demand different products, prices, service levels, channels, advertising and so on, as well as different methods of selling - in other words, a different marketing plan and eventually a different sales plan - and it is unlikely that salesmen working on their own at the 'sharp end' can determine these things in advance. Which is where well-organised marketing planning comes in.

For example, salesmen may be good at establishing friendly relationships with customers . . .

. . . but without the back-up of a well-organised marketing plan they are less likely to know which are the best groups of products or customers to concentrate on, to be able to plan their presentations well, to sell as confidently or to close the sale as effectively. Nor are their sales objectives likely to be as consistent with the company's marketing objectives as they should be.

Worse still, perhaps, marketing planners are often unaware of this. Too often sales and marketing are separate activities, with the budgets of the two reflecting this double-thinking.

In most companies, more money is spent on the sales force than on advertising and sales promotion combined, which is not surprising since they depend to a large extent on personal selling.

For instance, insurance companies need to discuss the details of individual policies with their customers, and this can be done best through personal representation; so personal selling is a vital and expensive element in the marketing mix, and has to be planned as carefully as any other element. So how do we go about it?

First the selling company must identify the *major* influences in the buying company on any purchasing decision. Then it must try to find out what each decision-maker needs to know at the various stages of the buying process. It will also need to know if the customer is buying for the first time or whether it is a repeat order. It's then possible to decide what part personal selling (and advertising, sales promotion, etc.) must play in all this.

The Advantages of Personal Selling

First, it's a two-way form of communication. The purchaser gets a chance to ask about a product or service.

1 ASK ME ANOTHER

IN YOUR PARTICULAR CASE...

2 Next, the sales message can be made more flexible and therefore more suited to the needs of particular customers.

I'M GLAD YOU ASKED ME THAT

3 Then the salesman can use the depth of his knowledge of the product to relate his products' benefit to the perceived needs of the customer.

The salesman can *ask for an order* and perhaps negotiate on price, delivery, or any other special requirements.

SO WHAT ABOUT IT, OLD CHAP? **4**

And, when this point has been passed, the salesman's task becomes one of re-inforcement, underlining the wisdom of the purchase and encouraging the customer to consider other products or services in the range.

NICE LITTLE MACHINE, THAT

A salesman is a person who, to the customer, personifies the company making the sale.

HI! I'M JOE!

EAT AT JOE'S

So personal selling is an essential ingredient in the marketing plan. Its value varies from market to market, but it must always be present. The salesman's role must be carefully considered in the sales plan.

But how many salesmen does a company *need*? However many there are they won't all be performing the same task in exactly the same way, at the same time. Opening new accounts . . .

. . . demonstrating new products, collecting debts, servicing existing accounts, etc. But there are cheaper ways of doing some of this.

SEE?

GNUH!

ACME JOKE & NOVELTY Co.

IT'S LIKE THIS...

Telephone selling perhaps - or debt collection by phone. The question is, are your salesmen using their expensive time to best advantage?

DO YOU HAVE TOO MANY SALESMEN WHO ARE NOT SELLING?

50%	24%	6%	20%
TRAVEL	MAKING THE CALL	SELLING	ADMIN

This is the workload of the salesforce of one major company. They found that their salesmen spent half their time getting to and from a call, 24% in making the call, 6% in actually selling and the rest completing the paperwork. This company was able to improve the amount of time devoted to selling by better planning and, to improve the quality of sales performance in the increased time available for meeting customers.

Salesmen's Objectives are QUANTITATIVE & QUALITATIVE

Quantitative objectives measure amounts.

There are obvious sales targets like "how many products sold?", "which products?", "which markets?". Other quantitative objectives might include statistics on display points, numbers of letters sent, telephone calls, reports, etc.

Qualitative objectives measure skills . . .

. . . e.g. the skill with which a salesman applies his product-knowledge to the job, or how he plans his work, how he overcomes objections during a sale.

Measurements of quantitative objectives are simple, whereas measurements of qualitative objectives are not. Qualitative measurements relate to *standards* of performance, i.e. efficiency, and the results of such measurements can lead to more profit for the company and higher salaries for the salesmen.

How do we manage the salesforce - increase their incentive?

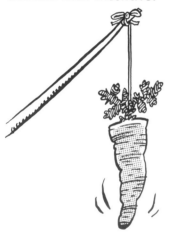

Remuneration for good performance is one way . . .

Rewarding extra performance attracts and keeps good salesmen and keeps the company competitive and rewards initiative.

But one of the most significant rewards for a salesman is the realisation that he's doing a worthwhile job, for a well-regarded company. So motivating the salesforce is a complex subject.

It's not enough for the sales manager, safe in his office to employ a combative manner. It is more realistic to *plan*.

MARKETING OBJECTIVES → MARKETING STRATEGIES

SALES OBJECTIVES → SALES STRATEGIES → SALES TACTICS

This means formulating a sales plan which is developed from the marketing plan. Sales objectives and strategies are the outcome of marketing objectives and strategies.

Co-ordination of the sales plan to the marketing plan will mean that the company's corporate objectives will relate more closely to customers' needs.

Sales tactics evolve from sales strategies and involve personal sales targets, route planning, acquiring new customers, etc.

Summary of Chapter 8

Sales force management and personal selling often suffer from neglect by marketing management, yet personal selling is a crucial part of the marketing process and must be managed as carefully as any other aspect.

Personal selling can be seen most usefully as a component element of the communications mix. A decision as to the role of personal selling in this mix can only emerge from the organization's thorough understanding of the buying process which operates in its markets. Research into buying decisions offers some help to organizations in achieving a suitable match between information required by the customer and that given by the company.

Particularly in industrial marketing, personal selling has a number of advantages over other forms of marketing communications; these should be intelligently exploited. There are three basic issues which must be resolved satisfactorily if the sales force is to operate in an efficient manner. The first issue concerns the number of salesmen needed. The organization should first establish the present pattern of work, then consider alternative ways of undertaking the tasks performed by salesmen. The next stage is to analyse the desired workload for each salesman and determine how the work, once measured, can best be allocated in terms of territory and time.

The second issue is concerned with the objectives of the job of the salesman. Sales objectives can be either quantitative or qualitative. Quantitative objectives are mainly concerned with what the salesman sells, to whom he sells it, and at what cost. Qualitative objectives are related to the salesman's performance on the job.

The third issue is the overall management of the sales force. Supportive modes of management are superior to repressive modes of management.

Chapter 9
The Pricing Plan

Nobody in business disputes the need to put a price on what a company sells, but the strange thing is that very few companies regard pricing a subject worthy of a plan of its own.

In fact, pricing is one of the four essential ingredients of the marketing mix, but it is rarely found in a marketing plan. The reason is that whereas the other ingredients can be measured *separately*, pricing is often an integral part of the offer. However, as we'll see, pricing is complex and worthy of being discussed separately although (like the other ingredients) it inter-relates with everything else in the marketing plan.

Here's a built-in problem about pricing . . .

Accountants and marketing men traditionally have differences in attitude about it. Marketers sometimes disregard the *short term* financial consequences of their decisions, believing in the value of *market share* to establish long-term market control.

On the other hand, accountants do not always understand the complex decisions about human nature which are involved in marketing, believing always in profitability on current trading, with prices often being set on some pre-determined cost-plus basis.

But the marketer knows that demand only exists at a price, and above that price a product will not be bought. Pricing then is an important factor in how successfully a product will sell.

So, accountants and marketers are sometimes fundamentally at odds, although when they do recognise each other's point of view they make a formidable team. Even so, given perfect harmony in a company, the problems of pricing are still complex.

It had three models, each regarded by the management as quite separate entities which appealed to different market segments. When one of the products - say, model A - became unprofitable it was thought impossible to open up new markets for it because the investment involved would make the model even less profitable. One of the reasons for this impasse was the firm's accounting system which was based on *current* production and distribution methods - a system which inhibited change.

The only course open to the firm was to put the price up. Result: even lower sales, and the model had eventually to be scrapped. The trouble was that all assumptions were based on the *existing* set up, rather than on a planned development. This is the kind of reasoning that has led to the decline of many companies.

Whereas Japanese companies were more prepared to make an effort to increase their market share, often by cutting their prices in order to achieve a long-term pay-off.

Such a strategy, however, is not appropriate in all circumstances.

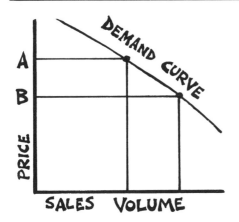

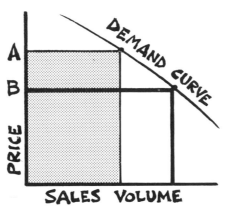

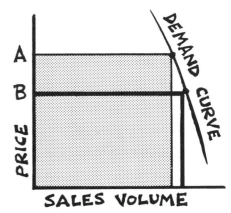

Let us assume there is a market where the demand curve looks something like this. Two firms, A and B, compete for the market with comparable products. A charges more than B. B sells more than A. Whose revenue is higher?

In other words, is area A (shown shaded) bigger or smaller than area B (shown with a heavy line around it)? The steeper the curve - in other words, the less price-sensitive the market - the more circumstances favour A.

B's area becomes appreciably smaller than A's. The steepness of the demand curve now means that the increase in sales for product B won't compensate for the cheaper sales price. So the shape of the demand curve has a fundamental effect on pricing, and this shape is likely to change . . .

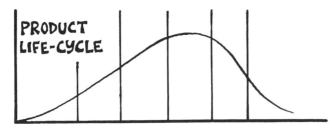

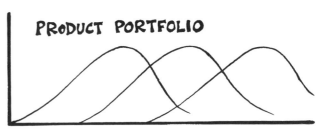

. . . as you will remember from the product life cycle which shows differences in price sensitivity throughout its length. The link between pricing and product life cycle becomes even more important in companies which have more than one product.

This means that a pricing policy has to be worked out for the whole product portfolio. The need for this is illustrated by the Boston grid we came across earlier.

MARKET GROWTH

Star	Wildcat
Cash Cow	Dog

MARKET SHARE

During its life cycle a successful product will progress from the wild-cat through the star stage and ultimately become a cash-cow. During that process the earning capacity of the product rises.

MARKET GROWTH

Star	Wildcat
Cash Cow	

MARKET SHARE

It moves from a position where it did not repay its investment to a position where it did - a process that might have taken years. Today's cash-cows finance today's wild-cats which in time become cash-cows themselves, and the process is repeated. Therefore . . .

DON'T PRICE INDIVIDUAL PRODUCTS IN ISOLATION

A   B   C

Marketing objectives for each product can vary from short-term profitability in some cases to an improvement of market share in others.

JAM TODAY.. ..AND JAM TOMORROW!

And so the pricing plan must take account of the role individual products play in the corporate strategy of the company. Next . . .

THE 'NEWNESS' OF A PRODUCT HAS AN EFFECT ON PRICING

BANG FRIZBANG -BANG FRIZBANG

I WANNA! GIMME! GIMME!

When a product is new, and also during the high growth phase of the product life cycle, price tends *not* to be the customer's primary consideration. Demand is high.

! GIMME! I WANNA! GIMME!

WIZBANG

But other manufacturers might wait for the market to be created, come in late and offer a competitive product at a lower price.

Now for another factor in pricing policy . . .

THE PRICE OF A PRODUCT SHOULD RELATE TO ITS PERCEIVED VALUE

Price is one of the most obvious indications of the value that is placed on a product. An article that can obviously command a certain price will be viewed with suspicion if priced conspicuously low.

So in many fields such as luxury goods, price is taken as an indication of quality. Getting this relationship right is called *product positioning*.

But if two products are not luxury products, obviously more or less the same, and do the same job, the cheaper product will probably sell better, especially in mature markets. In this case, other ingredients of the marketing mix must then be used to create consumer preferences.

PRODUCT: SAME

PRICE : SAME

PLACE : 24 HOUR DISPENSING MACHINES

PROMOTION: 'OUR SNAKE OIL WILL MAKE YOU FEEL 20 YEARS YOUNGER'

Here the manufacturer of one brand of snake-oil is using a round-the-clock distribution system and an appeal to a basic anxiety to set it apart from the competition. It's an attempt to disguise the similarity between this product and the competition.

So, an effort to build brand loyalty, particularly through advertising and sales-promotion is a way of blurring the distinction between similar products. It is a response to competition - always a threat and therefore an important factor in pricing policy. So is *potential* competition.

For instance, a company might develop and launch a new product, giving it a high price-tag to recover heavy investment costs, but by doing so providing a high *price ceiling*, or umbrella, for anyone else who cares to compete in this market.

Competitors who may well have benefitted from the original company's research and development may launch similar products at a much lower price, capturing a large share of the market and gaining valuable production experience. If Alpha had asked a lower launch price it would have retained the initiative, built a large market share and rapidly gained the experience to make the launch price profitable. Potential competitors would think twice about entering the market.

COSTS : ANOTHER IMPORTANT FACTOR IN A PRICING POLICY

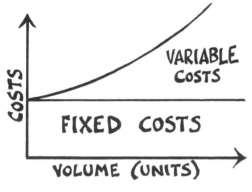

Many companies relate prices and costs like this. First they calculate fixed costs like overheads and salaries. Then they add variable costs. These will go up as the volume of *production* goes up.

The relationship between costs, profit and revenue can be illustrated in a break-even chart, like the one below.

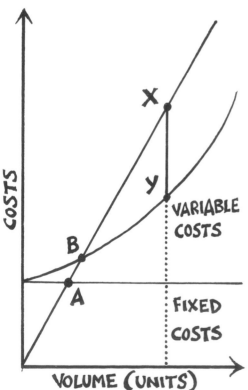

Then a *revenue target* is decided on for a certain volume of units produced. This will determine the price per unit. The revenue line intersects the fixed costs line at A. At this volume of production sales will only cover fixed costs. As the volume (and the revenue) goes up, the line passes through the variable costs line at B, so revenue will cover both variable and fixed costs. Above this point the product moves into profit, X representing the target revenue. XY is the line representing the profit margin. Sales might depend heavily on the price charged. To sell at too low a price would have the effect of making the revenue line less steep, in turn making the profit margin XY smaller and perhaps disappear altogether. This chart also illustrates the dangers of selling at either too high or too low a price. Too high and sales might be too low even to reach the fixed costs line. Too low, and whatever the sales volume, revenue might never meet variable costs.

The variable costs have been shown here as an upward curve, increasing as the unit volume increases. In fact with experience the cost of producing any one unit generally comes down, This is because of something called 'the experience effect', which means that a company gets more efficient as it gains marketing and production experience, and as it refines its manufacturing and distribution processes. The result is that the ratio of costs to *cumulative* volume decreases.

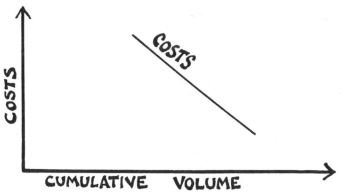

This is generally true of all competing businesses; so as products go through their life cycles both the real cost and the market price come down.

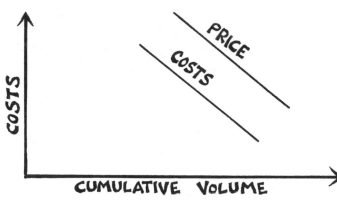

In this keenly competitive situation it's necessary for the cost reduction at least to match the reduction in market price.

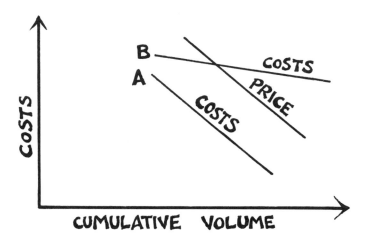

Here, company B is unable to keep its costs in line with the reducing market price, whereas its competitor A can; so B will find itself in trouble if it continues to sell at a loss in a mature market. We can illustrate the relationship between pricing and cost in simplified terms by considering the following two contrasting pricing policies.

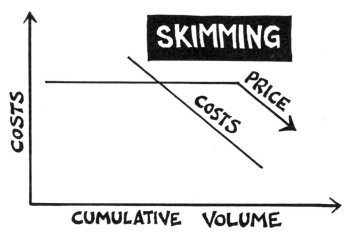

The first, called the *skimming policy* is one in which the price of the product starts high, then reduces in pace with reducing costs.

At the other extreme is the policy called *penetration*.

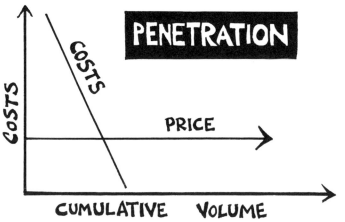

Here the price starts low, that is, the product is initially unprofitable, but as the product rapidly penetrates the market by under-selling the competition, sales volume increases and so does the company's experience. Costs are reduced at an even greater rate as time goes on and the product soon becomes profitable.

SKIMMING | PENETRATION

A skimming policy will tend to create an umbrella, or high price ceiling which will allow the competition to come in . . .

JAM TOMORROW

. . . whereas a penetration policy starts at a loss in the hope that the experience curve bringing costs down will allow the product to become profitable. Jam today versus jam tomorrow.

A Skimming Policy

has advantages where price is *not* an important consideration, and where production and marketing costs are not known.

A Penetration Policy

has its advantages in highly competitive markets where price matters.

But companies nearly always have a *range* of products, so the costing and pricing problem becomes more complex.

Here is a product range. *They are not all equally successful.*

We sell lots of these — all of them at a loss.

We sell a fair number of these, but the profit margin is low.

We don't make many of these, but each one makes a good profit.

If times are hard it is tempting to scrap the pyramids. The trouble is that, for cost accounting purposes, high volume products like this are often allocated the highest proportion of the company's fixed costs, and getting rid of that product wouldn't save all of these costs. So extra costs would have to be heaped on the others, and there's a good chance the cylinders would become unprofitable too.

What's more, the scale of the company's operations would shrink. It would become less efficient, with less investment incentive. It could waste away and ultimately go broke. So that's another complication. Now, finally, let's see what happens when a company uses intermediaries to distribute its products.

THE DISTRIBUTION CHANNEL

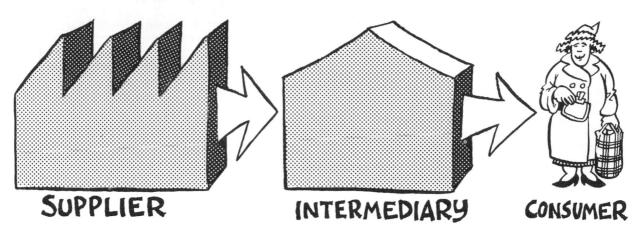

SUPPLIER   INTERMEDIARY   CONSUMER

Intermediaries - such as wholesalers, distributors and retailers - can be more efficient than the supplier at bringing the goods and the consumer together. Of course, they expect to be rewarded for their services, the reward being the margin between the ex-works price and the price to the consumer. We call it the channel margin - the channel in this case being the distribution channel.

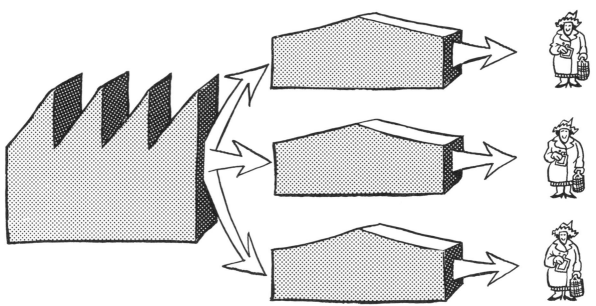

Unfortunately, the total channel margin may have to be shared between several intermediaries. The pricing problem here is how to give everyone a reasonable return and still keep the price to the consumer competitive. Circumstances give some distributors more bargaining power than others, making the business of calculating margins (and therefore prices) more difficult. How does the supplier reward the intermediary? He gives discounts.

DISCOUNTS

Trade

Quantity

Promotional

Cash

Here are four ways of offering discounts, none of them mutually exclusive. Trade discounts are offered to distributors who hold inventories of the supplier's stock and in effect re-distribute the products. Quantity discounts are offered to intermediaries who, as the name suggests, order in large quantities. *Promotional* discounts encourage distributors to share in the product promotion; and cash discounts of about 2½% are offered for prompt payment of bills.

Management of the channel margin depends on the best use of discounts and their most appropriate application to individual distributors.

Summary of Chapter 9

Pricing decisions are of paramount importance in marketing strategy. Like the other elements of the marketing mix, the price of the product should be related to the achievement of corporate and marketing objectives. Thus, the role of price must be established in relation to such factors as the product life cycle, the requirements of the total product portfolio and sales and market share objectives.

The procedures and methods adopted to meet these goals are as dependent on the market and competitive circumstances as they are on costs. Indeed, the market-oriented approach to pricing sees costs as a constraint which may determine a lower limit to the firm's pricing discretion rather than as a basis on which price is determined.

Getting the price right has a direct effect on revenue and profits. Almost by definition, the price of a product determines the profit margin, that is, the difference between the cost of producing an item and the price at which it is eventually sold.

But price also has a bearing on the actual quantity of product sold - since a higher price can reduce demand, while a low price can often lead to increased sales.

The margins given to intermediaries in the marketing channel should be viewed in terms of the *value added* by them as the product passes through the channel. In return for the performance of various functions necessary to the efficient completion of the exchange process, the organization will be willing to make available some of the total channel margin available to it. The various types of margins that are commonly encountered are trade, quantity, promotional and cash discounts.

REMEMBER:
The pricing policy of a product depends on the newness of the product, on costs, on its perceived value, and on your method of distribution

...and above all it shouldn't be done in isolation from all your other products.

Chapter 10
The Distribution Plan

In this chapter we're going to concentrate on that part of the Marketing Plan concerned with distribution, which means more than the *physical transportation* of goods. Product distribution divides into three main inter-dependent areas.

We'll take physical distribution and marketing channels in turn and then show how they relate to the output of the total system: customer service. First; physical distribution.

Physical Distribution | **Marketing Channels** | **Customer Service**

Physical distribution is one of the vital ingredients of the marketing mix. It is a major element of *place*. Its importance can be demonstrated by taking the average cost of a £1 sale, computed nationally.

DISTRIBUTION COSTS 21p

PROFIT 4p

MARKETING COSTS 27p

MANUFACTURING COSTS 48p

Roughly a fifth of the cost of a product goes on getting it to the customer. There will be exceptions of course, but, broadly speaking, this figure is representative enough to argue that distribution is a very important ingredient in the marketing mix. It is obviously important too in the entire trading process - in the business of getting the right product to the right place at the right time.

Here's one kind of distribution - the distribution of finished goods or services. Another kind is the distribution system which feeds the raw materials to the manufacturer, and there's also the *internal* distribution which occurs within the supplying company itself. This chapter concentrates on the distribution of finished products.

The first question to ask is: who is in charge of distribution?

Unless there is a formal distribution structure, it could easily be spread across production, marketing, finance and so on. Such an arrangement has obvious disadvantages - one distribution decision acting against the interests of others.

A more formalised distribution structure will make it more probable that all the distribution-related activities will not conflict with each other. Such an inter-related distribution system is often referred to as "logistics" in which one distribution activity is traded off against another to arrive at the most efficient system overall. For instance . . .

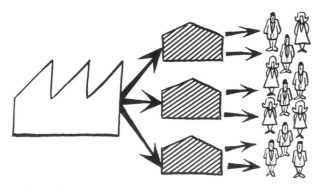

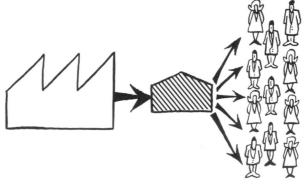

One physical distribution system might involve a number of field warehouses involving a combination of transportation modes in supplying the market.

Another system might involve fewer field warehouses and a different transportation mix.

This kind of trade-off is easier to make if it is the responsibility of one person or department without vested interests. Such a person might be called the Distribution Manager, and his options are ingredients in the *Distribution Mix*. There are five ingredients.

**FACILITIES
INVENTORY
TRANSPORT
COMMUNICATIONS
UNITISATION**

These five ingredients make up the total *cost* of distribution within a company. Here's what they mean:

Decisions about *facilities* involve, for example, the number and location of warehouses and plant - the problems associated with existing locations and decisions about new ones in response to changing demand. More field locations mean lower transportation costs but higher investment and overheads - one kind of trade-off.

Inventory

The problem of holding stock in anticipation of demand is a major item in distribution cost. Interest charges, deterioration, shrinkage and the necessary insurance and administration of adequate inventory are all items to be considered against having the goods on hand to meet the demand.

Transport

Important factors in transport decisions are concerned with the modes of transport required, whether to own or lease vehicles, delivery schedules, etc. Of the five ingredients in the distribution mix this is the one which gets the most attention, perhaps because it is so obvious.

Communications

But this ingredient is of equal importance, because without an efficient communications system, heavy additional costs may be incurred in other areas of the company because of poor order processing, inaccurate invoicing, etc. A satisfactory customer service depends on effective communications support. Bad communications can result in emergency reactions to unexpected demand, in dissatisfied customers and loss of trade.

Unitisation

This ingredient in the distribution mix concerns the way in which goods are packaged and grouped for handling, and it can have a major bearing on the economics of distribution. For example, the pallet can become the unit load for movement and storage; and container transport has already revolutionised both domestic and export transportation.

These five areas - Facilities, Inventory, Transport, Communications and Unitisation - constitute the *total cost* of distribution within a company.

Now let's look at the *marketing channels* through which a company reaches its customers - getting the right products to the customer at the right time.

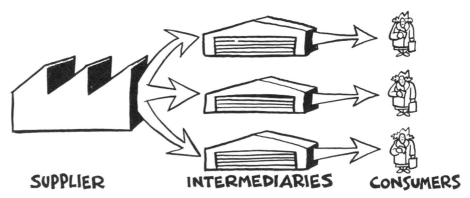

SUPPLIER   INTERMEDIARIES   CONSUMERS

Remember from the last chapter that some businesses put some or all of their distrubution in the hands of intermediaries, which affects the pricing policy of the company. It has the obvious effect on distribution (costs and management too), not only in the way the goods are physically transported, but in the change of title to ownership of the goods. The physical path may well be different from the one taken by the process of exchange of money for goods; particularly as many intermediaries share in the financial risk with the supplier. The supplier might well face a choice of marketing channels.

Some Choices of Marketing Channels:

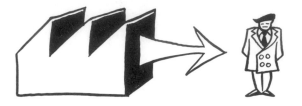

The supplier might want to supply a customer direct, perhaps by post or personal delivery.

He might supply to a wholesaler who in turn supplies a number of retailers.

He might distribute his goods through a retailer.

He might even appoint an agent, particularly in export markets.

Intermediaries are representatives of the supplier in the eyes of the customer, so it's important to evaluate each one carefully - Does he sell to our target market segment? Does he measure up to our own standards? Is he located well enough? Is he carrying competing lines? And so on.

The third area of the Distribution Plan is about Customer Service, the main components of which are consistency of order cycle time, effective communication between supplier and customer, and level of availability.

The ultimate purpose of any distribution plan is to make the right goods available to the customer at the right time, which is easy to say but frequently difficult and complicated to realise. To make available enough of every product to meet every conceivable demand at every sales outlet at any given moment would probably ruin the company. The difference in cost to the company of providing a 75% service and 100% service is enormous.

Costs of maintaining Customer Service

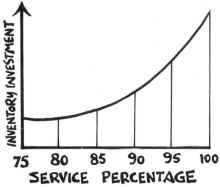

It would cost up to five times as much in inventory to supply 100% of the goods at the right time compared to a 75% service level of availability. So, what is the *right* level of availability of your services or products?

Theoretically you should try to maintain the highest level of availability you could possibly manage while staying in profit; but the truth is that customers are less aware of the differences in levels of availability as these levels get higher.

As availability approaches 100% the level of demand does not increase enough to make the extra investment worthwhile. So, a balance must be found between the costs and benefits involved in customer service. This point of balance is when the costs equal the extra revenue gained by the extra level of availability.

What does 'Customer Service' mean?

Broadly, it's the service provided to the customer from the time an order is placed until the product is delivered. But it's more than this.

It encompasses every aspect of the relationship between a manufacturer, his intermediaries and his customers; so it includes price, product range, availability, after-sales service, sales representation . . . in other words, the total activity of providing a service to a customer. This chapter is concerned only with the distribution aspect of all this.

Distribution is the cornerstone of customer service; but customer service often varies with each market segment. This will mean designing different customer service packages for different market groups, so it's necessary to work out what is important for each segment, and design a competitive package and promote it promptly.

The package will have to be piloted and monitored in the relevant market. Perhaps several packages will have to be made. Don't forget, in a competitive market, distribution becomes a vital factor. It could make the difference about who gets the order. So how does a company go about designing an efficient distribution system?

First, it may be the best policy to appoint a distribution manager instead of leaving it to the marketing manager. Distribution can involve complexities of labour relations, wage bargaining, technical problems, etc. and the immediacy of such problems could distract the marketing manager from his main job.

The function of the distribution manager is to integrate all the factors involved in moving goods from source to user.

SUPPLIER   WHOLESALER   RETAILER   CUSTOMER

Where do we start the planning process? As before, we conduct an audit, and as before, it's in two parts.

INTERNAL | & EXTERNAL

The internal audit will take account of such things as sales distribution, seasonal patterns, new products, packaging, transportation, storage, the pattern of data flow, inventory, manufacturing systems and so on - all the characteristics of the company which affect its distribution needs, in fact. The external audit looks at the market, distribution policy in regard to channels, the competition, government regulations and outside associations like industry groups, Chambers of Commerce and so on, who could help or hinder the distribution of goods.

FOUR BASIC OBJECTIVES OF A DISTRIBUTION PLAN

1. Objectives related to outlet penetration.

2. Objectives related to inventory.

3. Objectives related to distributor sales and promotional activities.

4. Objectives related to customer development programmes (e.g. incentives for distributors).

Finally, the Distribution Plan must be integrated with the Overall Marketing Plan

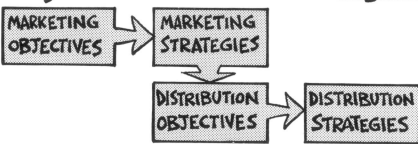

Once again, the distribution plan will flow from marketing decisions contained in the marketing strategy of the company. In arriving at distribution objectives, it's first necessary to evaluate changing conditions in all levels of distribution, relate the tasks involved to the overall marketing strategy, determine the distribution policy about type, number and levels of outlet, set performance standards and carry out checks to make sure the plan is working. All of that is contained in the distribution strategy.

Summary of Chapter 10

Where customers buy products is determined by the outlets at which those products are made available to them. The planning of the organization's distributive activity should be based on a careful assessment both of the market requirements and the ability of the firm to meet those requirements. The marketing channel through which products move is a network of institutions which themselves are linked by a series of mutually beneficial relationships. The marketing channel is itself dynamic, as are the markets that it serves. Accordingly, decisions regarding the choice of channel should be seen as an integral part of the firm's marketing strategy, subject to change and adjustment in the light of circumstances.

Getting the product to the customer cannot be viewed by marketing management as the concern of others. The distributive activity of the firm is as much a part of its marketing mix as are pricing, promotion and product decisions. Indeed, in some markets, the impact of the distribution effort upon sales can exceed that of the other mix elements. The implications of this view of distribution's marketing role are wide-ranging and involve a reappraisal of attitudes as well as of the means of distribution generally employed. The key to the successful development of the firm's distribution effort is the adoption of a total systems approach whereby an integrative view is taken of the various activities involved in distribution.

The output of such an integrated system is customer service. The task implicit in the management of customer service is to achieve a balance between the costs of service and direct customer benefits. The appropriate level of availability, which is the principal component of customer service, depends not only on profitability, but also on the nature of the product-market competition and the channels used. The customer's perception of logistics performance can be described as the customer service package.

REMEMBER:
If we have it in stock it'll cost you extra

Chapter 11
Marketing Information, Forecasting & Organisation

So far, this book has been concerned with the various elements that go to make marketing planning what it is. Now we're going to start looking at how to make it *work*.

We've seen that, in essence, the marketing planning process is simple, consisting of five steps, from the formulation of corporate objectives to the marketing planning programme itself. But the reality is more complex . . .

There are differences between individual businesses, and even in any *one* company the nature of its business is constantly changing. The roles of individuals within companies need defining, and departmental responsibilities in the planning process need to be agreed.

PUT IT OVER THERE, LADS.

MARKETING PLAN FRAGILE

PUT IT OVER THERE, CHAPS.

'When to plan', 'how often', 'by whom' and 'how' are all considerations unique to one company and one situation . . .

JAM TODAY

JAM TOMORROW

AND THE DAY AFTER THAT

. . . and there must be a relationship between short-term and long-term planning. So, the process may be easy, but the implementation of the process can be complex by virtue of its *context*.

The implementation of a marketing planning system is governed by two major constraints.

INFORMATION AND ORGANISATION

INFORMATION

In the first part of this chapter we'll concentrate on information flows and on forecasting. Later we'll look at the ways marketing planning systems are organised. Profitable development in a company is dependent on accurate information.

I WANT TO FILL ROUND HOLES.

WE MAKE SQUARE PEGS.

CUSTOMER

SUPPLIER

Profit will only come from matching a company's capabilities with customers' needs, so it's important that there is a flow of information between the customer and the supplying company, and this is the role of *marketing research*, the research into marketing processes - not to be confused with *market* research, i.e. research about the markets themselves.

MARKETING RESEARCH

DATA → RELEVANT INFORMATION → INTELLIGENCE

The collection of data is only the first step in marketing research. Data must be given direction before it can become relevant information, and this information is only relevant if the company has some purpose in mind. Information allied to purpose is intelligence.

INTELLIGENCE & RISK

WHERE'S THE OTHER SIDE, I WONDER?

LONG JUMP

Where there is uncertainty about the outcome of any business decision, management is likely to hesitate. But with relevant information, the uncertainty is translated into a *measurable risk*

INTELLIGENCE CONVERTS UNCERTAINTY INTO RISK

by assessing the probability of the outcome. This activity is marketing management's most important task.

One problem faced by marketing researchers is the sheer abundance of information.

So much so that it becomes indigestible and remains unread. The marketer ends up working by hunch alone in order to get the job done.

Also, marketing information is *perishable*, like yesterday's news, and it is of no use if it does not reflect the current situation.

FIGURES FOR LAST YEAR

Also, the same information gleaned from two or more sources makes for at least one redundant amount of effort and expense. So, how much *should* we spend on marketing research? How do we know when we're getting value for money?

SALES

ALL THANKS TO YOU, TONY. (I THINK!)

Perhaps it's most easily identified by success - by the profit which was *probably* achieved through identifying marketing opportunities and through the avoidance of marketing failures. But at what price? How much of the firm's money must be put into marketing research?

DEVELOPMENT COST: £1 MILLION

Perhaps a crude yardstick might be to take, say, the development cost of a new product. There is uncertainty about its chance of success. This uncertainty must be turned into acceptable risk.

DEVELOPMENT COST £1M ESTIMATED CHANCE OF FAILURE 10%

If it turns out that the chances of its failing are 10%, it's worth investing 10% of £1 million, or £100,000 to help avoid this loss. Because the product's chance of success depends to a large degree on the state of the market and on the product's intrinsic merit, marketing intelligence can play its part in reducing the risk factor.

TWO KINDS OF MARKETING RESEARCH

EXTERNAL RESEARCH takes place in the business environment.

INTERNAL RESEARCH is conducted inside the company.

External research serves to support the *information* gained internally from sales reports, changes in the marketing mix and other relevant material.

TWO KINDS OF INFORMATION:

REACTIVE

Reactive information involves the market place and requires certain groups of people to answer questions.

NON-REACTIVE

Non-reactive information does not rely on data derived *directly* from the respondent, but requires the company to carry out its own audits.

REACTIVE TECHNIQUES

need the co-operation of the market place, and require certain groups of people to answer questions. So an important tool in the process of gathering reactive information is the questionnaire.

Three Kinds of Questionnaire:

Personally administered questionnaires

Phone questionnaires

Postal questionnaires

Personally administered questionnaires are the best controlled, but they are expensive and time-consuming.

Questionnaires conducted by phone are easy to organise and are relatively cheap and quick, but the amount and type of information gained is usually limited.

Postal questionnaires are also limited; not by the amount of information but by sample bias and possible lack of feedback. Also, the design of the questionnaire is most important . . .

It's important to avoid asking loaded questions. It should be able to provide you with the information you really need. Pilot testing with a sample population is therefore essential.

Depth interviews are particularly useful in specialised markets. The interviews are loosely-structured discussions within a relatively small group under the guidance of a group leader.

Another way of gathering information is by experimentation, by market-testing new products for their performance, or by testing different variations of the marketing mix.

NON-REACTIVE TECHNIQUES

do not involve the direct co-operation of the market place and are controlled completely by the company . . .

. . . e.g. by retail audits, in which the supplier monitors a representative panel of stockists . . .

. . . or consumer panels who record their purchases over a certain period. This enables the supplier to identify usage patterns of certain sections of the market.

But most of the useful marketing research is done at home in the supplying company, looking through existing materials, statistics, reports, newspapers, trade journals and so on. Information from these sources is very powerful when combined with the company's own sales information and other internal data.

So marketing information or data can be obtained from external and internal sources and is reactive or non-reactive in character depending on its source. It only becomes useful if given direction and allied to a purpose.

Now let's look at how we organise this process into a market intelligence *system*.

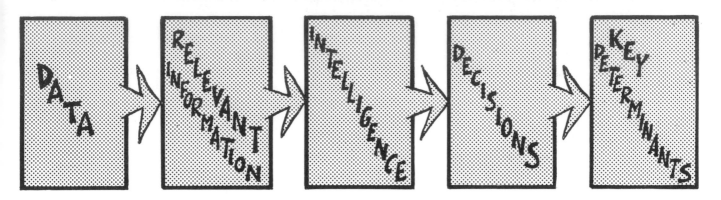

DATA → RELEVANT INFORMATION → INTELLIGENCE → DECISIONS → KEY DETERMINANTS

The success of this will depend upon the ability of management to identify marketing decisions and the information needed to make decisions. It's only possible to identify the necessary information if the *key determinants* of success are isolated - for example, the significance of market share or the correct service levels for profitable growth. There are four steps in the construction of a good market intelligence system.

- LIST DATA
- LIST DECISIONS
- COMBINE TO IDENTIFY REQUIREMENTS/PURPOSE
- ORGANISE SYSTEM TO ACCOMMODATE

First, make a list of all the current data and information available. Then get each manager to list the decisions he has to make together with all other relevant information. Next, combine all this and look for redundancies and overlaps in the information requirements. (A matrix is a useful way of doing this). At the same time identify the purpose of each requirement and write it down. Finally, there is the difficult task of organising a system which will allow you to achieve your purpose.

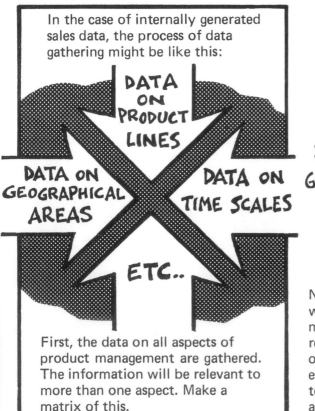

In the case of internally generated sales data, the process of data gathering might be like this:

DATA ON PRODUCT LINES

DATA ON GEOGRAPHICAL AREAS

DATA ON TIME SCALES

ETC..

First, the data on all aspects of product management are gathered. The information will be relevant to more than one aspect. Make a matrix of this.

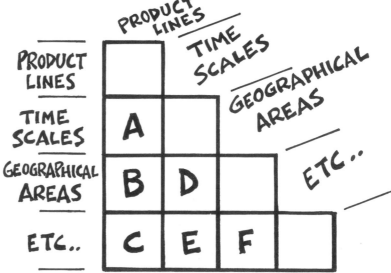

Now it's possible to identify a number of objectives on which to report; for example, in this highly abbreviated matrix a regularly produced product-line report might be in respect of performance information on time-scales (box A) or geographical areas (box B). The objectives and purpose of each report are then listed, and only then will it be possible to devise a marketing information system to accommodate all this.

DEVISING A MARKETING INFORMATION SYSTEM

Use a 'building block' approach, each block representing a sub-system for meeting a particular information need. Eventually a totally integrated system can be developed according to users' needs. Such a system could be expensive to set up and run, particularly as markets are constantly changing, so you will need to evaluate the probable cost of the system before embarking on something which might prove to be too costly, complex and time-consuming to maintain.

FORECASTING

The complexity and size of the marketing task facing businesses has grown in recent years. Customer needs are more diverse, resulting in shorter product life cycles. Diversification and internationalisation has meant increased competitive pressures. Socio-cultural, legal and political factors affecting the business environment are changing rapidly . . .

All this has meant that it's becoming more and more difficult to find and develop profitable markets.

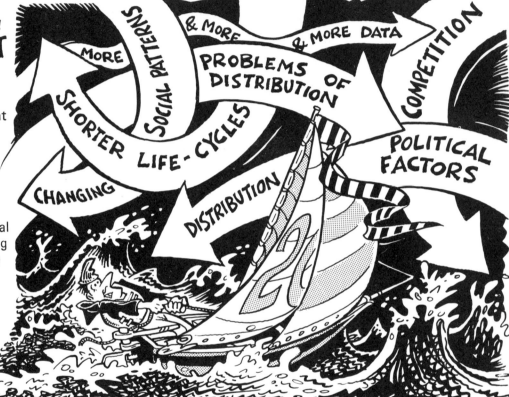

And this has made forecasting more hazardous and less accurate still. However, it remains a crucial activity, and getting your forecasting wrong could be disastrous.

So, what does forecasting entail?

MACRO & MICRO Forecasting

Before any company can set marketing objectives and strategies it must make some long range forecast of the total market. This we call *macro* forecasting. Then, after the company has decided what specific market opportunities it wants to take advantage of it must make detailed forecasts in respect of the various units within the company. We call these *micro* forecasts.

QUANTITATIVE and QUALITATIVE TECHNIQUES

I PREDICT 250,000 DARK STRANGERS WILL CROSS YOUR PATH WITHIN 5 YEARS

Macro and micro forecasting both require two kinds of forecasting technique. Quantitative techniques are based on statistical probabilites. But some forecasting needs to be qualified because the quantitative statement does not take into account likely changes in past trends. So after the quantitative forecast on the information available it's necessary to use qualitative methods like expert opinions, market research, etc. to predict likely discontinuities. Otherwise forecasting is likely to be inaccurate, and therefore dangerous.

UNFORTUNATELY, ONLY 10,000 WILL BE BUYING YOUR PRODUCT!

Organising for Marketing Planning

Each business has its own unique structure, so it follows that the structure of its marketing planning organisation will be different too. What's more, every company changes as it evolves.

MARIO'S ICE CREAM — A STOP-A ME AND A-BUY ONE

The business may start as a one-man organisation, with literally every activity - purchasing, advertising, manufacture, selling etc. performed by the same person.

When this happens, it's organised around the owner, who knows everything about the business. The organisational form can be represented like this:

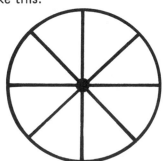

Formalised planning and written procedures are less relevant than in the case of larger companies where responsibilities are more diversified. As it grows, the one-man firm will meet an organisational crisis.

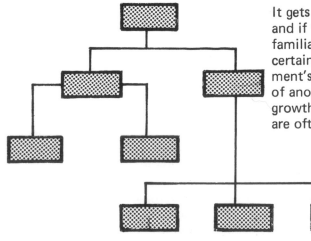

It gets more complex. The first organisational form breaks down, and if the company is to survive, the organisation evolves into the familiar pattern of a family tree, with certain functions allotted to certain individuals. The next crisis will happen when one department's decisions begin to have an adverse effect on the functions of another, which will especially matter if the firm is in a low-growth or stagnant market. It is at this point that serious attempts are often made to formulate marketing planning.

Companies which have arrived at this stage of evolution have a management structure like this:

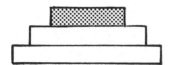

The top level strategic management is shown shaded, supported by its lower management levels. In a diversified company it gets more complicated.

Here some of the central strategic functions are repeated at the subsidiary level in the operating units, resulting in new products or services being introduced by the subsidiaries with their own markets in mind, without reference to headquarters. Unless some kind of planning is introduced, duplication of effort and conflicting strategies will result, with an inevitable drop in profitability. Some kind of *marketing system* is required. It will be quite different from the system where there is no *strategic* level of management in the subsidiary units.

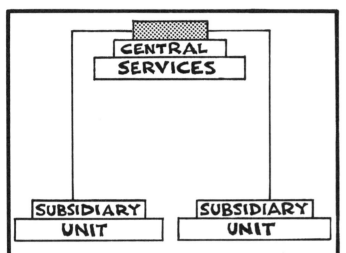

This organisation tends to lead toward standardised strategies; new products being designed with as many markets in mind as possible. The danger here is that the subsidiary units can become less sensitive to the needs of individual markets, and so less flexible and competitive. Another kind of marketing system is needed here. In both cases, the role of the central strategic management is crucial, in clarifying its boundaries and those of the business as a whole.

The role of marketing planning is to control and harness the growth of the company for greater profitability. At board level the relationship between *marketing* and *sales* is crucial.

Here sales and marketing are separated at board level.

The danger of this is that the real power is vested in the sales organisation, with marketing relegated to a staff activity. Of course, a strong chief executive can make sure the two activities are sensibly co-ordinated, but he may be too busy always to do this.

A better organisational system might be this:

The conflict between sales and marketing can now be resolved outside the boardroom, and what the marketing department is *planning* has some relevance to what the sales department is actually *doing* in the field.

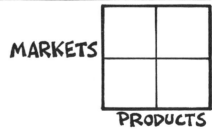

Another kind of conflict is inherent in marketing itself. The Boston Grid represents marketing as being concerned with combinations of products and markets. Organisationally, many companies have 'product managers' and 'market managers' with the result that the company orientates towards one or the other.

A Product-Manager-oriented company might well be weak in market knowledge, with the danger that many of their products become unsaleable.

On the other hand, a Market-Manager-oriented company might end up with unnecessary product differentiation and poor overall product development. So, a good marketing organisational system must take account of both products and markets. Finally . . .

Each Company must devise its own Organisational System

The following factors have to be borne in mind when designing the organisational system for marketing planning:

- MARKETING CENTRES OF GRAVITY
- INTERFACES WITHIN THE ORGANISATION
- RESPONSIBILITY
- COMMUNICATION
- CO-ORDINATION
- FLEXIBILITY
- HUMAN FACTORS

First, the company has to decide what its most important markets are; then how the various areas within the company react to each other, particularly departments like sales - which are concerned with *present* performance - and marketing which is concerned with the future.

Another important factor concerns who has responsibility and authority for making a marketing planning system work. Should it be a 'marketing planner', an overburdened line manager or even the chief executive?

How do areas and individuals communicate with each other? How are their efforts co-ordinated? How can the system be made flexible to take account of change? How can the strengths of individuals be used, and how can their weaknesses be accommodated for the good of the company?

Summary of Chapter 11

Marketing research is an integral part of the marketing task. It provides the manager with the means of identifying market opportunities, and it aids his understanding of marketing processes, and it can provide data for control of marketing programmes. Whilst marketing research will always be less than precise in that it deals with unstable behavioural phenomena, it nevertheless provides an invaluable means of contact with the marketplace.

Much valuable marketing information can be gained from the examination of existing data which may be to hand within the company or from published sources. Additionally, a wide range of techniques are available to the organization that needs to take a proactive approach to researching markets.

All estimates of markets and sales take place against a background of uncertainty caused by the ever-changing environment. Sales estimation must, therefore, be able to provide a flexible framework for marketing action and must recognize the probabilistic nature of forecasts. The central task of sales forecasting is the estimation of market potential and the share that any product might be expected to achieve, a task which is influenced both by the forecasting horizon and by the stability of the markets themselves.

The techniques for forecasting include both macro and micro approaches. The former include the use of marketing models and enable the forecaster to deduce from a broad economic analysis the implications for a particular product-market. Micro approaches are based on building up an estimate of sales from an individual customer level.

In organizational terms, the marketing department can usefully be seen as just one part of an integrated pattern of activities which is designed to achieve corporate goals. Marketing management must work alongside its colleagues to ensure that the organization's products meet present and future customer needs. Marketing should take place as close to the customer as possible.

Does your Dog like DOGGO?
YES ☐
NO ☐

REMEMBER: To make marketing planning WORK, you need INFORMATION, so that you can FORECAST the market, so that you can ORGANISE your business to cope

Chapter 12
Designing and Implementing a Marketing Planning System

In the last eleven chapters we've seen that the *principles* of marketing planning are *the same* whatever the size of the company. In this final chapter we'll deal with the way in which the structure of a company determines the character of its marketing planning system. All marketing plans have two major things in common.

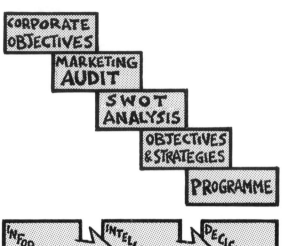

CORPORATE OBJECTIVES

MARKETING AUDIT

SWOT ANALYSIS

OBJECTIVES & STRATEGIES

PROGRAMME

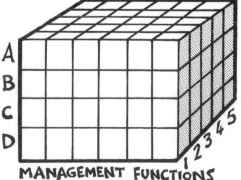

INFORMATION → INTELLIGENCE → DECISIONS

They all have the same structure - the five steps leading from the corporate plan to the formulation of a marketing plan . . .

. . . and they have the same system of implementation. Raw *information* is given direction; this information thus becomes *intelligence*, about which it is necessary to take the calculated risk of making marketing *decisions*.

This structure and system applies to small companies and larger organisations alike . . .

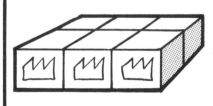

. . . and even to whole groups of companies. The objectives and strategies for different organisations may differ, and very large organisations or diversified groups will need a *number* of marketing plans for each part of the organisation.

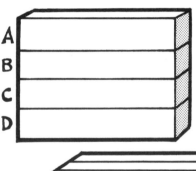

A
B
C
D

Here's an organisation which has a number of companies, here identified as A, B, C and D. These companies each operate in a number of regions.

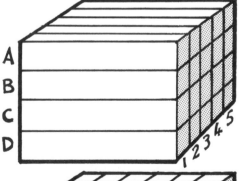

A
B
C
D
1 2 3 4 5

These regions are numbered 1, 2, 3, 4 and 5. Let us assume that each company has comparable management functions - production, distribution, sales, etc.

A
B
C
D
1 2 3 4 5

MANAGEMENT FUNCTIONS

And so the activities of this organisation can be represented by a three-dimensional grid. Let's take a marketing plan which encompasses all the functions of just *one* company, say Company A in all the regions in which it operates.

ALL REGIONS

A

ALL MANAGEMENT FUNCTIONS

1 2 3 4 5

The plan would relate to this part of the grid.

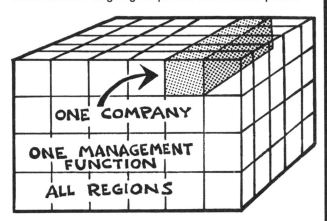

ALL COMPANIES, ALL MANAGEMENT FUNCTIONS

ONE REGION 2

In the same way a plan embracing all the companies in just *one* region would look like this. Such plans which relate individual organisations within larger groups we call *macro* plans.

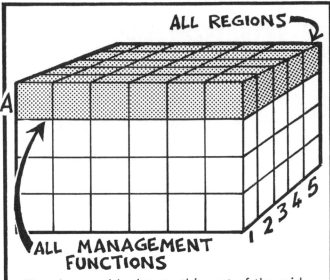

ALL COMPANIES, ONE MANAGEMENT FUNCTION, ONE REGION.

Marketing plans which deal with the operations at a more detailed level within the group we call *micro* plans. This is a micro plan for one management function (say, finance) which links the financial management of all the companies operating in one particular region.

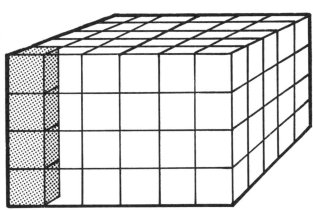

ONE COMPANY

ONE MANAGEMENT FUNCTION

ALL REGIONS

Whereas this micro plan co-ordinates the management of a common function, e.g. production in *one* company in *all* the regions in which it operates. This model serves to illustrate the fact that marketing plans are able to accommodate *all* kinds of organisations regardless of size or complexity, and that plans of varying sizes are needed to relate the activities of companies within the group. Obviously, however, only plans which are essential should be produced.

Two factors govern the degree of complexity within an organisation

SIZE
DIVERSITY

Size is an internal characteristic of an organisation. Diversity relates to a business's markets.

The least complex environment is one in which there are a limited number of markets, so an *undiversified* company is the least complex in marketing planning terms.

However, here's a large company whose product range is relatively undiversified, but which might have quite diverse markets. This will mean that the central function at Headquarters is almost as difficult as in a diversified conglomerate, even though it's likely that the top management will have more in-depth knowledge of the product range. Nonetheless, marketing planning is generally easier in this kind of company.

Here's another example of a large business - a company supplying electrical fittings to the automobile industry. The company might have a highly diversified range of products, but comparatively few customers. Again, marketing planning is likely to be easier in this case than in a truly diversified company.

Let's look at what marketing planning means to a small undiversified business.

Mario will need a marketing plan, despite the small size of his business, and its structure will not differ *in principle* from any of the plans needed by multinational corporations. But because he is smaller the way he implements his plan will be different. Size is the biggest determinant of the planning system used.

Mario has a high in-depth knowledge of the key determinants of success or failure. He's got a good knowledge of the technology needed and of the markets to be satisfied.

This knowledge is easily shared with Mrs Mario, the key subordinate who makes the ice cream he sells.

Because of everybody's day-to-day involvement there is less need for written procedures than there would be if Mario's firm was nation-wide. However, even at Mario's present stage of development the strategy will need to be explicit and the marketing concept understood.

But as companies get larger the operational problems get more complex. Top management is less likely to have in-depth knowledge of the business through informed processes and is less likely to react to day-to-day fluctuations in the market without written procedures.

In the end, this insensitivity to the needs of the market will result in frustration and the ultimate decline of the business. So the rule is: the bigger and more diversified the company, the bigger the need for standardised, formalised procedures.

But the question of sensitivity to the market place raises another question: who is to make marketing decisions? Should it be top management, who are remote from the scene, or those at the 'sharp end', who have intimate knowledge of the markets, but less corporate authority?

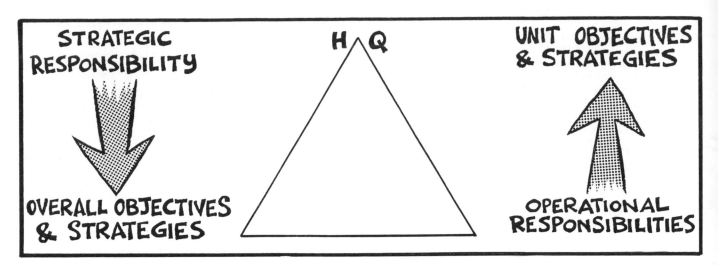

STRATEGIC RESPONSIBILITY

OVERALL OBJECTIVES & STRATEGIES

H Q

UNIT OBJECTIVES & STRATEGIES

OPERATIONAL RESPONSIBILITIES

In this diagram the pyramid represents a highly simplified management structure in a large organisation. Top management has strategic responsibility for such things as deciding on which products to develop, which markets to enter, etc. Top management is therefore responsible for setting corporate objectives and strategies and passing these down through the company, shown here on the left hand side of the diagram. But at the lowest management level there is a reciprocal responsibility, shown on the right. This is to communicate the objectives and strategies of each unit up through the company hierarchy. In this way the decision-making for *tomorrow*, which is the responsibility of top management, is interdependent with the decision-making for *today*, the responsibility of operational management.

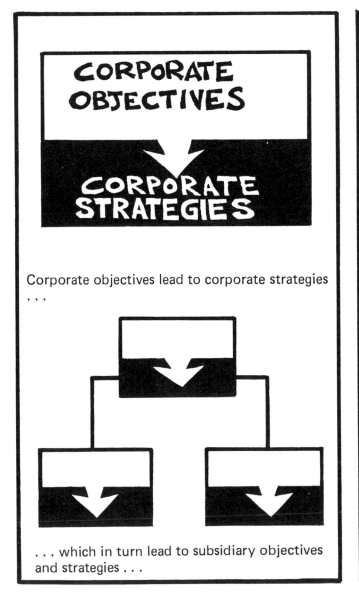

CORPORATE OBJECTIVES

CORPORATE STRATEGIES

Corporate objectives lead to corporate strategies . . .

. . . which in turn lead to subsidiary objectives and strategies . . .

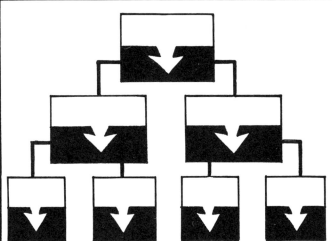

. . . and so on, down the line until the unit level is reached, with the communication process reciprocated back up to top management level. In this way even the largest organisation is able to evolve a series of marketing plans which will be flexible enough to contain a hierarchy of audits, SWOT analyses, objectives and strategies at the strategic level and at the same time have the local application needed at the operational level. Conglomerates can diversify their detailed objectives and strategies to each country of operation. This balance between the flexibility of operating units and centralised control is achieved by planning from the top down *and* from the bottom up, with some agreed procedures for trading off the legitimate interests of both levels. But as we've already seen, marketing planning must also be formalised to suit the size of the company.

Here are four outcomes of marketing planning, only one of which is right. In the first case, bureaucratic planning results in a highly formalised system with no scope for individual creativity or initiative. In the second and third cases, we see the two extremes; first, *anarchy* where there is complete freedom for the individual and no system; and *apathy* where there is nothing - no system, and no initiative. Finally, we see a system in which the balance is right between the requirements of some workable system and freedom for individual initiative.

Complete marketing planning will provide guidelines to management at all levels but will allow entreprenervial initiative within the system - but the *degree* of formalisation will depend on the company's size and diversity.

Let's look finally at the timescale of marketing planning and the conditions that need to exist in a company if an effective marketing planning system is going to work. Remember, the activity of marketing planning starts with a statement of overall objectives and strategies. These may then modify top management's view with the result that revised corporate objectives and strategies are made, so the system is an inter-reaction between overall management objectives and strategies and those at lower levels.

CORPORATE OBJECTIVES

MARKETING AUDIT

SWOT ANALYSIS

OBJECTIVES & STRATEGIES

PROGRAMME

STRATEGIC PLANNING LETTER

AUDITS OBJECTIVES STRATEGIES ETC..

REVISE OBJECTIVES, STRATEGIES, ETC...

H.Q

HQ CONSOLIDATION OF OPERATIONAL & STRATEGIC PLANS

PREPARATION OF SHORT-TERM BUDGETS & PLANS

In the first instance the chief executive issues a policy statement - here a strategic planning letter - outlining objectives in all important areas of company activity. From this follow a series of audits, SWOT analyses, objectives and strategies and budgets relating to the long-term plan, the most common being for a 5-year period.

These are processed upward through the management hierarchy, and this twin process will provoke an interaction resulting in possible modifications to the long-term plans. Once agreement has been reached on the long-term direction of the company, unit managers can start preparing short term plans and budgets - normally for one year.

Finally H.Q. will consolidate operational and strategic plans. The whole process will begin between ten and six months before the beginning of the following financial year.

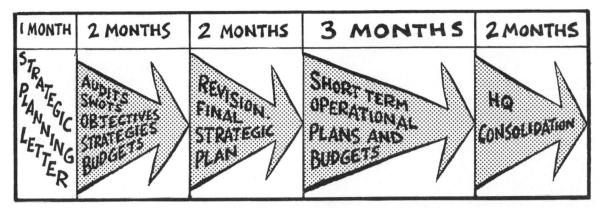

1 MONTH	2 MONTHS	2 MONTHS	3 MONTHS	2 MONTHS
STRATEGIC PLANNING LETTER	AUDITS SWOTS OBJECTIVES STRATEGIES BUDGETS	REVISION. FINAL STRATEGIC PLAN	SHORT-TERM OPERATIONAL PLANS AND BUDGETS	HQ CONSOLIDATION

In a ten-month planning system it might look like this with all the marketing and management audits, SWOT analyses, objectives and long-term budgets being initially undertaken in the second and third month. Then comes a crucial period of revision and re-evaluation of long-term objectives, strategies and budgets followed by the preparation of short-term operational plans and budgets.

The last two months are devoted to the consolidation of operational and strategic plans. Note particularly the inclusion of a time to revise and alter plans to take account of conflicting needs from different areas of the organisation and to give a flexible response to ever-changing market conditions. This is particularly necessary in very large organisations which can not respond as readily as small companies to the volatility of the market place.

CONDITIONS NECESSARY FOR AN EFFECTIVE PLANNING SYSTEM

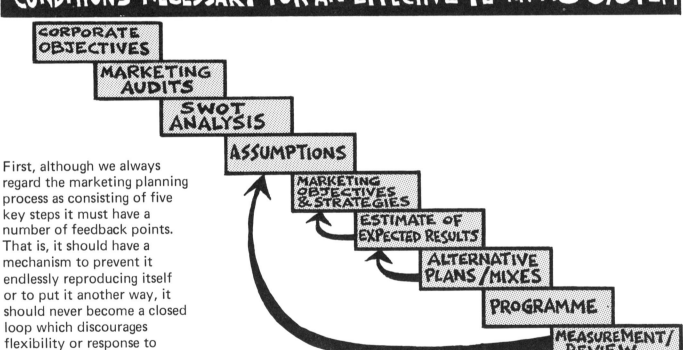

First, although we always regard the marketing planning process as consisting of five key steps it must have a number of feedback points. That is, it should have a mechanism to prevent it endlessly reproducing itself or to put it another way, it should never become a closed loop which discourages flexibility or response to change.

CORPORATE OBJECTIVES
MARKETING AUDITS
SWOT ANALYSIS
ASSUMPTIONS
MARKETING OBJECTIVES & STRATEGIES
ESTIMATE OF EXPECTED RESULTS
ALTERNATIVE PLANS/MIXES
PROGRAMME
MEASUREMENT/ REVIEW

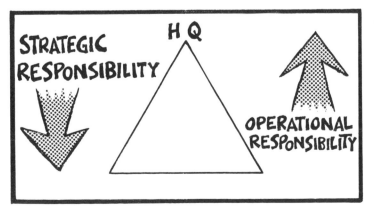

STRATEGIC RESPONSIBILITY
HQ
OPERATIONAL RESPONSIBILITY

The second condition for an effective marketing planning system is that planning at a functional or operational level should be integrated with strategic planning, and that planning at functional levels should be integrated with other functional areas so that one area's gain does not become another's loss.

94

Another condition is that the Chief Executive should take an active role in the planning and implementation of the system . . .

. . . and finally, the time scale for introducing an effective marketing planning system should not be under-estimated. In large diversified companies it can take up to three years. In smaller companies it should take less time; but even then it is not easy and will require training and lots of patience. But in the end, an effective marketing planning system will pay handsome dividends as many companies who have followed this programme will testify.

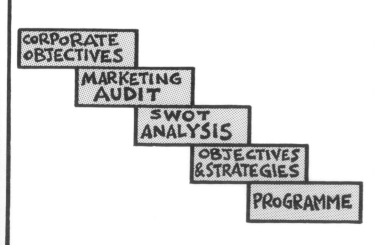

Essentially the process is simple in concept, consisting of five key steps in which it is essential that there is feed back and revision; but in practice it is complicated by the complexities and conflicts of need within individual businesses. There is, of course, no such thing as a ready-made marketing planning system. The most successful systems will result from adaptation to circumstances and, in the final analysis, from an understanding of the business of marketing itself.

· END ·

Summary of Chapter 12

REMEMBER:
Designing and implementing is a continuous two-way system

The major benefit of marketing planning derives from the process itself rather than from the existence of a formalized plan. This process is itself universal, irrespective of an organization's circumstances. However, what is not universal is the degree of formalization of this process, which will vary according to how big an organization is and the degree of product-market diversity.

One of the principal dangers in formalized marketing systems is the threat to creative thinking as a result of the accompanying bureacracy. Therefore, there has to be some mechanism for preventing inertia from setting in. The principal means by which such inertia can be avoided is the active participation of the chief executive and other key directors. The role of the chief executive is generally agreed as being: to define the organizational framework; to ensure that strategic analysis covers the critical factors; to maintain the balance between short and long term results; to display his commitment to planning; to provide the entrepreneurial dynamic to overcome bureaucracy; and to build this dynamic into the planning operation by motivating his key executives.

One of the key functions of marketing planning is to turn data and information into intelligence, which is information useful to and usable by executives in making key marketing decisions.

Marketing planning should happen at all appropriate levels throughout the organization, and it should be a continuous process rather than a once-a-year ritual.